Jewellery Making
for Profit

By the same author

Practical Jewellery Repair

Jewellery Making for Profit

JAMES E. HICKLING

NAG Press
an imprint of Robert Hale · London

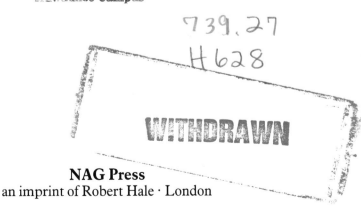

ISBN 0 7198 0092 7

Robert Hale Limited
Clerkenwell House
Clerkenwell Green
London EC1R 0HT

3 5 7 9 10 8 6 4 2

Photoset in North Wales by
Derek Doyle & Associates, Mold, Clwyd.
Printed in Great Britain by
St Edmundsbury Press Limited, Bury St Edmunds, Suffolk.
Bound by WBC Book Manufacturers Limited,
Bridgend, Mid Glamorgan.

Contents

Illustrations

Introduction

The essential difference between making jewellery for pleasure and making it for profit is the speed of manufacture. Some people are so gifted that they can design and make a piece that is original and beautiful which obtains a price that is out of proportion to the time and effort that went into the making of it. That is one way of making jewellery for profit. For most of us it is a matter of coming up with an idea that sells, then devising the means of manufacture that is efficient enough to leave a profit margin after all the costs have been deducted.

It is possible to manufacture items entirely by hand and make a profit if you can sell them direct to the public but that usually means having your own shop with all its attendant overheads, and running a shop does not leave much time for manufacturing.

At the other end of the scale you can lay out several thousand pounds on a complete casting outfit capable of turning out almost finished items in large quantities but that puts you in competition with all the people who have already done it and are well established so unless you can come up with a new slant you are at a considerable disadvantage.

This book is intended to take you along the middle road by speeding up the hand making process with the use of simple home-made punches, dies and jigs. Anyone who is capable of making jewellery by hand can make the simple tools described here.

As it is impossible to know the abilities of a potential reader, it is difficult to decide what to include and what to leave out of a book like this so one has to err on the side of caution and include some explanations that the more experienced reader will find tedious, to them I apologise.

For
Maggie and Jo

1 Workshop and Equipment

No matter how much workspace one starts out with in any craft it can become insufficient with the passage of time. If a three by five metre room seems adequate in your estimation – double it, because in six or twelve months time it will be full to overflowing with equipment or material you had not thought you would be using or needing. Like a version of Parkinson's Law: equipment expands to fill the space available.

It is the same with power points, lights and windows: the more you have the better. The limit is often set by the cost of heating the premises, so whatever compromise you arrive at make sure it is the best possible.

A similar law applies to workbenches, unless they are built to generous proportions to begin with they eventually end up being too narrow or too flimsy or the space beneath wasted due to bad planning.

If two rooms are available it is preferable on health grounds to reserve one for polishing, cleaning and gilding and any other process that creates excessive dirt, smells or poisonous fumes. A sink and extractor fan can be sited in this room to cope with the hazards.

A very convenient way of constructing workbenches is by using Dexion or similar pierced metal strips. They can be made rigid and strong but at the same time easily modified when necessary and you do not need an 'A' level in joinery to construct them.

An ideal surface for benches of this construction is the 30mm thick Formica covered chipboard sold at DIY stores for use as kitchen worktops. The tough hardwearing surface is immune to oil also any precious metal filings can be recovered from it with the minimum of loss.

All jewellers acquire a range of hand tools best suited to their method of working and the processes they favour most. The following list of hand tools is given because it includes a few that are more common to the engineer than the jeweller but will be needed to make the numerous small tools and machines described in the book.

1 Piercing saw
2 Blades for above. 2/0, 3/0, 4/0
3 6'' hack saw. (Handysaw)
4 12'' (30cm) Hacksaw frame
5 High speed steel (HSS) blades for above
6 Ringmaker's file. 6'', cut 2
7 10'' (25.5cm) half-round medium cut file
8 Set of 4'' model maker's files
9 Range of needle files
10 Broaches, assorted
11 Hand-reamer. 5/16'' or 8mm HSS
12 Set of HSS twist drills up to 3/8'' or 10mm
13 Set of taps and dies. HSS up to 3/8'' Standard Whitworth or metric equivalent
14 Micrometer. 1'' or 25mm
15 Ring size stick
16 Triblet. (Tapered mandrel)
17 Ring clamps
18 Heavy bench block, steel. 6'' by 4'' approx
19 Three pairs of 'AA' tweezers
20 Spring dividers
21 Three pin vices, assorted sizes
22 Two pairs of straight pliers. (Jeweller's type)
23 One pair of parallel jaw pliers
24 One pair of round nosed pliers
25 One pair of ring pliers
26 Tinsnips
27 Jeweller's hammer, 2oz
28 Ballpein hammer, 4oz
29 Planishing hammer
30 Lump hammer, 2lb
31 Hand brace
32 3½'' Engineer's vice
33 Emery paper. 1M, 4/0

34 Engineer's blue
35 Bottle gas torch. (Propane). Sievert size jets numbers 3537, 3939, 3941
36 Pendant drill
37 Assorted burrs

MACHINERY

Polishing machine. This should be minimum ½hp, preferably ¾hp, 3000 rpm. If long runs are anticipated which entail the operator working for half-an-hour or more consideration should be given to the more expensive machines used by the dental trade because, if well mounted, they are virtually silent

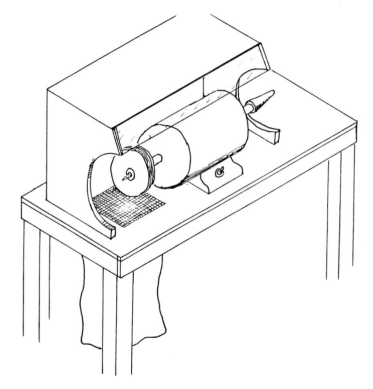

1   Home made dust extractor for a polishing machine. The transparent strip above the motor is acrylic sheet

and as they are completely sealed eliminate the need to keep the ventilation slots free of fluff.

Unless some form of dust collector is fitted dust will quickly spread over the whole workshop. A purpose built unit with extractor fan and collector box is the ideal but they are expensive. The home made set-up shown in fig. 1 works quite well. The fan can be an ordinary domestic extractor fan providing there are no ventilation slots for the dust to get in. It is mounted below a hole 15cm diameter covered with wire mesh. An old pillow case makes an excellent dust bag. The method of fixing it below the bench must be reasonably air tight if it is to work efficiently.

Rolling Mill. A hand-operated one with step down gearing

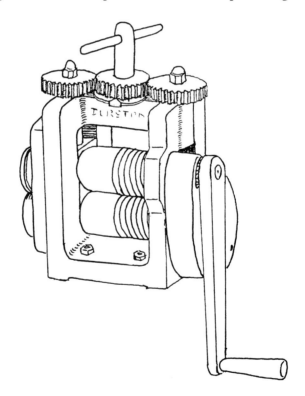

2   Rolling mill with reduction gear and extensions for
supplementary rollers

and suitable for both wire and sheet with extensions to the main rollers to accommodate supplementary rollers is adequate. Fig. 2.

Grinder. This need not be a heavy-duty model as it is used mainly for sharpening small tools and drills and sharpening the edges of small press punches.

Drill Press. There is a range of small, bench mounted drill

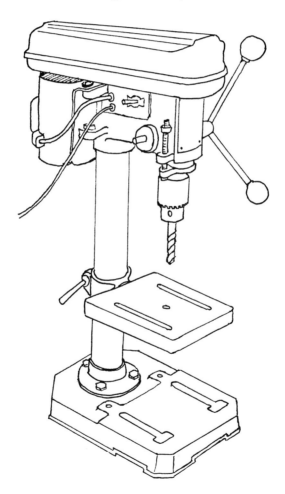

3   A typical bench mounted drill press

presses now on the market retailing for less than a hundred pounds. Though a lot of drilling work can be carried out on the lathe, or bench mounted power drill, they are no substitute for these neat little machines. Two things to watch out for when buying are: some give out a noisy rattle when in use due to a poorly fitted spline on the driven pulley and the jacob type chuck has very slack jaws which means you have to be very careful when inserting a drill to be sure that it is clamped in the centre of all three and not between the sides of only two.

Guillotine. This will save you struggling with tin snips on metal that is too heavy for them or wearing out your arm muscles with a hacksaw. As always the largest you can afford and accommodate is the best.

Pinfold Ring Sizing Machine. There must be a lot of these

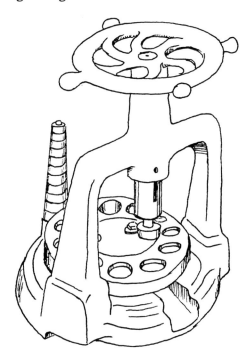

4   Pinfold wedding ring sizing machine

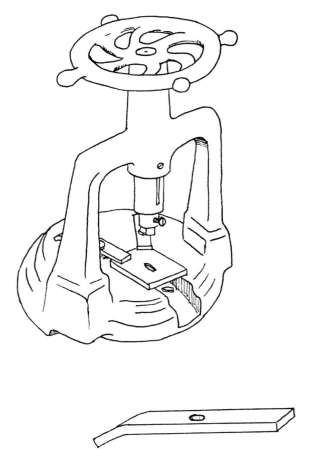

5   Pinfold machine adapted for use as a simple press

still around, probably tucked away in a corner of the workshop and forgotten having been replaced by more modern inventions. If one can be rescued, a few simple modifications can turn it into an excellent light duty press for stamping out small items. Fig. 5.

Bench Vice. A heavy duty version with 3½'' (90mm) jaws similar to the design in fig. 15 is best.

Fly Press. It has nothing to do with the winged variety, the fly

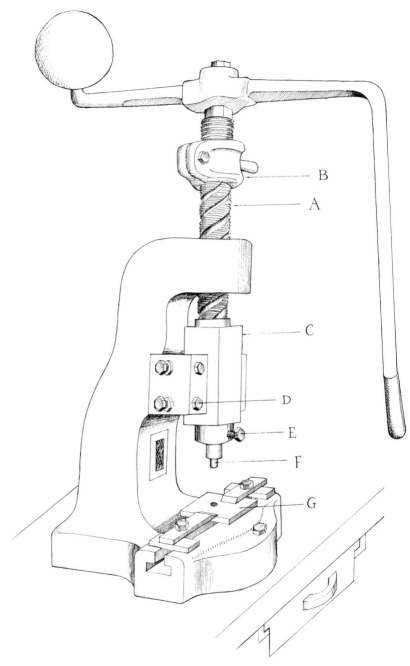

6 Number two fly press. A. Screw   B. Clamp   C. Slide   D. Slide
adjustment   E. Punch clamping screw   F. Punch   G. Die

is the large iron ball mounted on the cross arm to add power to the blow. They come in a range of sizes, the one illustrated in fig. 6 is a number two and is a good general purpose machine for jewellery work. It is approximately 30″ (75cm) high and takes up about a two foot square (60cm) of bench space but it requires a little more space than that for the arm to be swung. Secondhand ones are readily available from machinery dealers and can be picked up quite cheaply. The slide 'C' is adjustable so any wear can be taken up but the screw and its female counterpart are not so check them for wear. A little bit is tolerable but if you have to move the handle more than a couple of inches before the screw begins to travel look around for a better one. Do not be misled by play in the housing that couples the screw to the slide, wear at this point can be taken up by the use of packing pieces.

Fly Press in use. A simple punch and die for stamping out small circles are shown in fig. 6 F & G. In use the punch is fitted into the holder at the bottom of the slide and the clamping screw tightened. The die plate is then laid on the base and lined up with the punch and the punch lowered until it enters the hole in the plate. While in this position the plate clamps are moved along the 'T' slots until their ends rest on the die plate. They should not overlap the plate more than is necessary to clamp it firmly, in this case about a ¼″ (6mm). If they project too far on to the plate they will interfere with the metal being stamped. Next place a metal packing piece, ideally the same thickness as the die plate, under the tail of plate clamp to span the 'T' slot and provide a support for the clamp. Then tighten down the clamp screws a little at a time by hand so that an even pressure is applied to both sides of the die plate. Uneven pressure can result in the plate moving while in use and becoming chipped or even broken. Another cause of disaster is small particles of metal between the plate and press base so be sure to give both a wipe before setting up. Finally tighten the clamp screws with a spanner then lower the travel clamp 'B' until it rests against the top surface of the press. Raise the punch by moving the operating arm a quarter of a turn and lightly oil the punch and the hole in the die plate. Select a waste piece of the metal, similar to that you are going to be working on and place it over the hole in the die plate.

Now swing the operating arm in the opposite direction driving the punch through the metal.

Keep a piece of thick cardboard handy and stamp a few discs out of it to clear the metal disc out of the hole in the die and into the drawer below. If the press is correctly adjusted the piece of scrap material will have been pushed only on to the tip of the punch and a slight downward pressure will release it. If it is further up the punch it will be difficult to release even if the punch was well oiled and you can waste a lot of time freeing it so adjust the travel clamp until the punch just cuts the disc and no more. When you have got it right tighten the nut on the travel clamp and you are ready to begin stamping.

If the punch enters the hole in the die when you set it up but only indents the metal instead of cutting out the disc this is usually due to a bit of wear on the screw and you will have to adjust the travel clamp until the punch cuts through.

At this point always check that the die clamps have remained firmly in position and that the die plate has not moved. That first blow usually exposes any maladjustment caused by particles of metal trapped beneath the die plate or clamps. Check again after a few blows because hours of work can be lost if the punch fouls the die plate chipping one or the other. Also check the punch clamping screw as the vibration may sometimes loosen it. This may not cause damage to a round punch but certainly would to any other shape.

If a particular punch and die is going to be used a great deal and for fairly long runs they are often fitted into a die set and clamped firmly and permanently in position. This eliminates the need to adjust the machine every time it is used and removes the possibility of misalignment. It also enables an added refinement to be fitted in the form of a stripper which is usually a thinner duplicate of the die plate through which the punch passes; on its return journey the stripper pulls the metal off the punch.

The die set, fig. 7, usually consists of two accurately machined plates of cast iron held together by a pair of spring loaded guides. In use the whole unit is clamped into position in the press and the travel clamp set to allow the punch to enter the die as before.

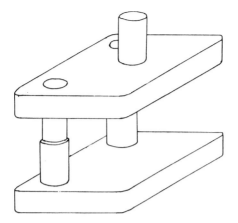

7 Small die set used for permanent and accurate alignment of punch and die

Lathe. Most of us gained some familiarity with the lathe at school; it is the simplest of machine tools to operate and the most versatile. Only the simplest of turning operations will be required to make most of the small tools described in this book, i.e. reducing the diameter of a section of round bar and drilling an accurately centered hole in the end.

For those not familiar with its use there are several booklets available from M.A.P. publications which will explain the modest skills required.

A model maker's lathe or instrument maker's straight (non-screwcutting) lathe will be adequate but a larger one is capable of taking heavier cuts quickly and of handling larger work should the need arise. Secondhand lathes are readily available but if the headstock bearings are not adjustable or all the adjustment has been taken up they are pretty useless unless you are capable of replacing the worn parts.

The model maker's lathe shown at fig. 8 has the various parts labelled. Taking them in turn from left to right. The headstock contains the mandrel revolving in two precision bearings; it is driven through either gears or pulleys and a belt by an electric motor. It is essential to have a hole through the centre of the mandrel so that bars longer than the depth of the chuck can be held and turned, the larger the hole is the more useful it will be.

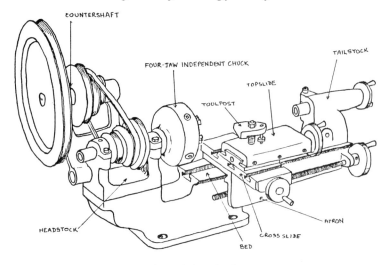

COUNTERSHAFT
FOUR-JAW INDEPENDENT CHUCK
TAILSTOCK
TOPSLIDE
TOOLPOST
HEADSTOCK
APRON
CROSS SLIDE
BED

8   A model maker's lathe

The distance between the centre of the mandrel and the top of the bed is known as the centre height and this is usually quoted as the size of the lathe. A good general purpose lathe for a jeweller would have a centre height of around 10cm. The length of the bed is the other crucial dimension because the two together govern the maximum diameter and length of what can be turned. Because the majority of large diameter objects that have to be turned are short disc shaped items some lathes have a smaller centre height but have a gap in the bed at the mandrel end to take large diameter work. This makes for a smaller, lighter and consequently cheaper machine without too much loss of capacity.

The hole at the front end (nose) of the mandrel is tapered for the first 6 to 10cm depending on the size of the bore. This is called a morse taper and various tools can be bought that have a matching taper on the shank. If they are ground very accurately they will form an extremely tight bond when placed one inside the other, powerful enough to resist the twisting action of a large diameter drill. They are numbered according to size and the size of lathe we are talking about would have either a number one or two, the latter being the larger.

A new lathe is usually supplied with a face plate, a pair of centres and a driving dog. The face plate screws on to the nose of the mandrel and large or awkwardly shaped items can be bolted to it to be turned. When the centres are placed, one in the mandrel and one in the tail stock, a bar with matching centre holes drilled in each end can be held between them. To rotate the bar the driving dog, a circular clamp with a protruding leg, is clamped to the bar just in front of the face plate and engages with a short rod bolted to the faceplate.

A much more convenient way of holding the workpiece is with a chuck. The one shown is a four-jaw independent chuck. They come in various sizes, the size being the diameter of the body. A convenient size for a 3½'' lathe would be 15cms (6''). As the name suggests the jaws can be moved individually so as well as round objects it can hold odd shaped and sized ones as well. Its jaws are reversible so it has only one set. It can do anything that the self-centering chuck can do and a lot more besides but it takes a lot longer to centre round items, so, if you have to choose have the four-jaw independent, but if you can afford it have both.

Three-jaw self-centering chucks always have two sets of jaws stepped in opposite directions, one set for smaller diameters of work and gripping cylinders from the inside and the other for larger diameters.

They are opened and closed by a scroll engaging with teeth on the underside of the jaws. The scroll is turned with a removeable key which fits into a square hole on the side of the chuck. The scroll, teeth and slideways wear with use and the chuck gradually loses its accuracy so if a turned piece of work has to be removed from the chuck and replaced later for further work always mark the work adjacent to one of the jaws before removing it and note the number of the jaw, which is stamped on it, then it can be replaced in the same position and lessen the chance of inaccuracy in the subsequent turning. A 10cm (4'') is a good general purpose size but the size of either will be dictated by the size of the lathe.

Most lathes have an attachment that screws on to the nose of the mandrel to enable it to accept collets. These act like miniature chucks of extreme accuracy but each can hold only one size of bar, the maximum size being governed by the size of the hole in the mandrel. For the size of lathe in question this would be 10 or 12mm. They are more commonly found on instrument and watchmaker's lathes where such accuracy is essential and are used almost exclusively when working on round bar.

There is often an arrangement of gears in the headstock of lathes of this size called a backgear. With the operation of a lever or pin this gives an additional range of very low speeds, which is necessary when turning very large diameters, and also enables the mandrel to be locked in position which is useful if keyway cutting needs to be done.

The saddle straddles the bed of the lathe and is able to slide back and forth along it on accurately ground ways. It is usually driven by a handwheel mounted on the apron of the saddle which turns a pinion whose teeth engage in a rack running the length of the bed. On small or cheap lathes this is done more slowly by a screw running the length of the bed which engages in a nut in the saddle and is turned by a handwheel at the tail end of the lathe. The more expensive lathes have both devices and the nut is split so that it can be disengaged from the screw when not in use. It is used on this type of lathe, in conjunction with an arrangement of gears, for screwcutting or giving an automatic traverse to the saddle. The cross-slide runs on a dovetail slide and is moved at rightangles to the bed by means of a handwheel. It has several 'T' slots machined in its surface to enable the top slide or other accessories to be bolted to it.

The part of the top-slide that is bolted to the cross slide usually has some means of rotating it through a number of degrees and locking it there so that it can be used for turning a range of short tapers. The cutting tool is held rigidly to its surface by an adjustable clamp or up to four tools in a four-way toolpost. Either type are usually called the toolpost.

The tailstock can be moved to any position along the bed and locked in position. It carries an extendable barrel which is directly in line with the mandrel whose movement is controlled by a handwheel at the rear. The inside of the barrel has a morse taper to take a centre, drill chuck or other accessories.

Cutting Tools. For all general purposes high speed steel is used for the cutting tools. The tools can be bought ready ground to shape or in short, square section pieces you can grind to shape yourself. In 1868 Robert Mushett discovered an alloy of steel containing carbon, tungsten and manganese that would harden when only air cooled and would maintain that hardness even when worked at high speed when high temperatures were generated. Before that water quenched carbon steel tools were used and you can still make your own tools from that material but if used on anything harder than brass will soon lose their cutting edge.

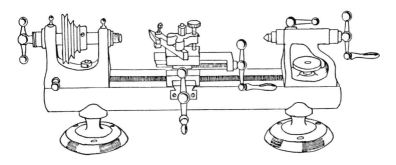

9   Instrument maker's or straight lathe

The most commonly used cutting tool shapes are shown in fig. 9a. They are, from left to right, a Right Hand Knife Tool, Round Nosed Tool, Boring Tool and a Parting Off Tool.

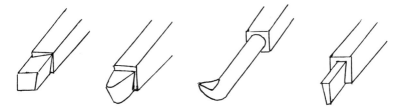

9a   The most commonly used cutting tools

The first is for all general purpose turning. The top face of the cutting edge should be at an angle of 10 to 15 degrees to the horizontal for steel but much less for brass and the vertical face ground to a slight angle as shown. For maximum efficiency there are different angles quoted in engineering books for different metals, and different alloys, but if you are doing lots of small jobs on differing materials you will soon find what is the best compromise.

The round nosed tool is for imparting a fine finish to a

turned piece. The boring tool is for enlarging the diameter of a drilled hole or squaring off the bottom of a drilled hole. The parting off tool, as its name implies, is for cutting the workpiece off when the turning is finished. Working with this tool on brass usually presents no problems but on steel even when plenty of cutting oil is applied often has a tendency to dig in. If the sides are ground at a slight angle so that only the cutting edge is in contact with the workpiece the risk is reduced. A further precaution is to cut two overlapping slots each a little at a time and also reducing the speed often helps.

All these tools should be set with their cutting edges at dead centre height, if they are higher they will rub rather than cut and if set lower the workpiece has a tendency to climb up on to the cutter.

MATERIALS

Steel. A range of silver steel round bars – known as drill rod in the USA – will be required from a diameter of 3mm (⅛'') up to 20mm (¾''). This material can be hardened and tempered easily and is available from many hardware and model maker's shops and advertised in model maker's magazines. It usually comes in 30mm (12'') lengths. It is very accurately ground to size and will fit perfectly into a reamered hole of the same diameter.

Gauge plate is the name given to the flat, accurately ground bars of the same material. One strip of each of 3mm x 50mm (⅛''x2''), 5mm x 50mm (3/16''x2''), 6.5mm x 50mm (¼''x2'') will cover most requirements. Where accuracy does not matter old files can be used as a make-shift but they require annealing then filing to remove the teeth.

There are two types of mild steel commonly available: bright mild steel and hot-rolled steel. The latter is cheaper but has a hard scale on it and is generally used for welding work where the finish is not important. Bright mild steel is the same material with the scale removed and rolled to a very close tolerance. In all cases where mild steel is mentioned in the book bright mild steel should be used.

Hardening and Tempering. Mild steel does not contain a

large enough percentage of carbon to allow it to be hardened in the normal way. It can have a hard skin formed on it by heating to bright red and then rolled in some high carbon compound such as Kasenit. This forms a shell around it to prevent oxidation. It is then reheated to bright red and quenched in cold water. This process can be repeated to obtain a thicker hard skin but the mass of the material beneath will remain soft.

Silver steel already contains this additional carbon so can be hardened throughout by heating to bright red and quenching in cold water. To be more specific bright red is sometimes described as cherry red and sometimes as carrot red. In my experience cherries come in a variety of shades so I should stick to carrots. Above that colour the term yellow red is used. At this heat the metal becomes more brittle and is liable to crack when quenched. When it reaches the hardening colour it should be held there for a short time, enough for the whole piece to reach uniform heat then plunged quickly into the water. Care must be taken not to allow cutting edges or sharp corners to become overheated or they will become brittle. If too much time is taken between removing the flame and quenching it will be less hard and a scale will form on the surface. When it is in the water it should be agitated until cool to prevent steam bubbles forming on the surface, and in cavities, causing uneven hardening and sometimes cracking. A useful tip that appears to work is that delicate die plates are less likely to crack if plunged into slightly warmed water. In theory this should make them less hard but I have never found them to blunt any faster than when plunged into cold water and I have never had one crack since doing this. Coincidence?

Tempering is controlled softening to remove brittleness and give the steel the working properties you require. If a clean piece of flat steel is heated from one end at one point there will be a range of colours from medium blue, purple, orange to yellow. The yellow is usually termed straw colour and in all the cases mentioned in the book that is the colour to aim for when tempering. The steel is gently heated with a soft flame until it is this colour then quenched again. It is sometimes difficult to get a uniform colour over the whole piece in which case heat the non-working portion first and quench when the cutting part becomes straw coloured. The darker colours are used for woodcutting tools and the blues for springs.

A propane torch with a large jet will cope with all the hardening and tempering work described here. It can be turned on full blast for the hardening and turned down to give a bushy flame for the tempering. Torches that burn a mixture of town gas and air are just as good. Oxy-acetyline is such a concentrated flame that it is difficult to get the steel to a uniform heat but it can be done with practice.

It is much easier to get a uniform heat if it is heated in a bed of granulated charcoal or pummice, or failing that, on a fire brick but slightly raised up on small broken pieces with a few larger pieces forming a surround to keep the heat in.

Copper. Copper has always been a popular material for jewellery, partly because of its beautiful colour and ease of working and partly because of the firm belief that many people have that it eases the symptoms of rheumatism and arthritis if worn as a bangle or ring on the affected limb. It is also relatively cheap and available in finely finished sheet, tube and wire.

Bangles and rings in this material are nearly always open ended because to solder them would create so much more work in finishing that the resultant price would be out of all proportion to their sales value. This also eliminates the need for a range of sizes as the article can be opened or closed to fit the wearer.

I will explain first how to make a simple copper bangle entirely by hand then show how each operation can be speeded up considerably by simple machines, tools and jigs. The same explanation would apply to the making of a ring which is only a bangle on a smaller scale.

A bangle to fit a large number of average sized wrists would need to be 16.5cm long and a comfortable width would be 2cm. If it is made from 1mm thick metal it will be pliable enough to slide over the knuckles and spring back into shape and strong enough to keep its shape for a long time. Copper sheet is available in the annealed state or what is called 'half-hard'. The latter is the best for all jewellery purposes, it has just sufficient springiness without being too hard to work easily.

If the strip is cut from the sheet with tin shears the edges will be burred and distorted and will have to be flattened by hammering with a mallet on a smooth metal bench block or passed through the rolling mill as described later. Go easy with the mallet because even in the half-hard state it is easy to mark it. When it is flat take off all the sharp edges and corners with a file then polish on both sides.

Though a plain bangle would be quite acceptable it does show up the slightest mark and scratch therefore a patterned finish would make it more durable and appealing. The most common form of patterning on copper is planishing which means completely covering the surface with light blows from a hammer with a slightly convex surface. The more rounded the face of the hammer the smaller the indentation it leaves, consequently the more hammer blows needed to cover a given surface.

Special planishing hammers with hardened and polished surfaces can be purchased but any small hammer with the working surface rounded and polished with extra fine emery paper will do just as well though you may have to repolish it every so often.

The bench block or whatever surface is used to support the workpiece must be perfectly smooth as any imperfections will be transferred to the back of the workpiece. This work should be carried out on a heavy solid bench in order to deaden the

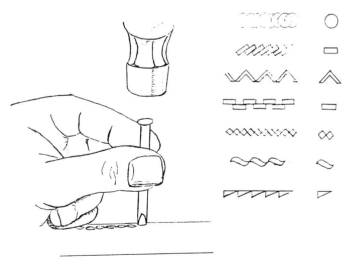

10   Samples of punched patterns

noise and vibration as much as possible. Keep the blows even and avoid going too close to the edge of the workpiece otherwise slight bulges will result which will have to be filed away afterwards. It does not take long to develop a rhythm with the hammer and to get the blows exactly where you want them.

As an alternative to planishing there is an infinite variety of punched patterns that can be created using punches made from nails. A selection is shown in fig. 10. The ordinary mild steel that nails are made from is hard enough to mark half-hard copper and should they wear can be easily sharpened with a file. Hardened masonry nails can be used as an alternative but they can only be shaped with a grindstone which limits the variety of designs.

Another method of decorating copper is by engraving. Though it is a highly skilled trade on its own it is not beyond the average person's ability to create simple designs on copper which is one of the easiest metals to engrave and on which engravers learn their trade.

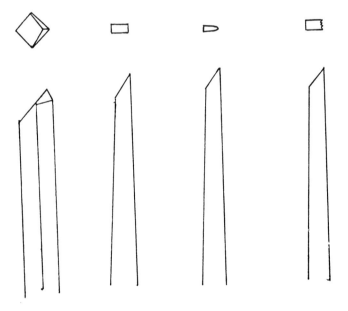

11 Most commonly used gravers. *Left to right*: square graver, square scorper, dotter also used for stone setting and a stitch or liner

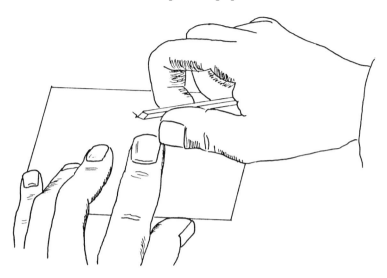

12   Holding the graver

A selection of gravers is shown in fig. 11 and fig. 12 and shows how the engraving tool is held.

The square graver is the one most commonly used but it takes a fair bit of practice to sharpen it correctly and guide it round a cut. It helps a bit if the tip is lubricated with a thin grade of oil as copper tends to be a sticky metal to cut.

By far the easiest way of engraving on metal is to use the flat bottomed graver and wriggle it. To do this the tip of the graver is pressed lightly into the metal then rocked from side to side and moved forward at the same time, a little like you would move a wardrobe across a room; you would tip it one end and 'walk' it. There is a tendency at first to tilt the graver more in one direction than the other but if you watch your hand while you are doing it you can detect and correct it. Using the tool in this way it is easy to engrave curves and create a variety of patterns and designs and used in conjunction with punches the variety is endless. See fig. 13.

Always draw the lines that the graver must follow with a scriber beforehand because what you have already engraved is hidden by the graver and your hand making it impossible to get repeated patterns to match. Designs can be drawn on paper first then transferred to the copper with carbon paper

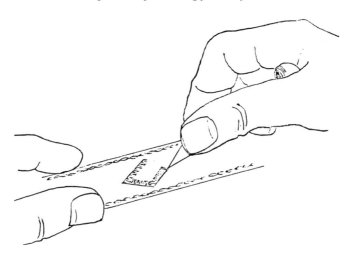

13　Wriggling with a square scorper

and then marked out with the scriber.

Engravers usually support large workpieces such as this on a small leather cushion filled with sand. A beginner would find the bangle much easier to handle if it is stuck on to a small piece of board with shellac or double sided adhesive tape then supported on a leather cushion or some similar object that will raise it above the bench surface and allow it to be swivelled about easily.

Matt finishes can be created in several ways. For creating small matt areas within a design a matting punch is best and they are so cheap it is hardly worth making one yourself. Larger areas can be covered using a steel wire brush mounted in the polishing machine. Most hardware shops stock these in various grades as they are used for rust and paint removal. The finish will consist of a series of fine lines travelling in the same direction. A more matt and less directional finish can be obtained by using a special matting brush obtainable from jewellery tool dealers. These consist of a number of loosely mounted steel wire bristles on a central hub. When rotating centrifugal force makes the bristles stand out like an ordinary steel wire brush but when they strike the surface of the metal being treated their loose mounting allows them to bounce off instead of being dragged across the surface and the finish is akin to sandblasting.

Another device for mounting on the polishing machine, and also available from hardware shops, consists of a series of squares of coarse emery cloth mounted around a wooden hub. The finish it gives is similar to a wire brush but without the danger of steel bristles flying off and hitting you in the face.

Yet another way to matt the surface of copper is to lay it on a strip of new emery cloth and pass it through the rolling mill a couple of times. You are restricted by the width of the rollers and must take great care that no grains of emery remain on the rollers afterwards or find their way into the bearings.

Finally there is sandblasting itself but this requires a separate machine and an air pump so unless you are using it quite a lot it is difficult to justify the expense.

Another decorative finish can be created by oxidizing the surface of the copper using copper sulphate or liver of sulphur. A small quantity is dissolved in warm water and the items immersed in it. The oxide takes best to a scratchbrushed or slightly matt surface. The oxide is dark brown in colour, the depth of colour depending on the time it has been standing. If left too long the colour becomes very dense and brittle and tends to chip or flake off. A bit of experimentation will show what the best colour is. This operation is best carried out in the open or beside an extractor fan because the solution gives off a powerful smell of rotten eggs.

There are many preparations available for oxidizing copper and brass giving a range of tones from black, grey and brown to dark green. Some are used as a paste that can be applied to specific areas while others are applied by immersion.

A two-tone effect can be obtained by polishing the oxide away in certain areas. On a planished surface the high points will show the colour of the copper and the indented hammer blows will retain the oxide giving a very attractive result.

It is always necessary to give copper jewellery a coat of lacquer because it oxidizes very quickly when exposed to the atmosphere. It is not like the even browns induced by sulphur products but a patchy discoloration which is unattractive.

Clear cellulose lacquer is the usual one used as it is durable and very quick drying. It can be applied in three ways: brushing, spraying or dipping. The last is the best and cheapest for jewellery. It is usually of a treacly consistency when purchased and needs to be diluted so that the excess will not run off to form thick edges and blobs at the lowest parts when hung up to dry, nor so thin that an insufficient coating is left on the article. There is nearly always a small drip suspended at the bottom but this can be touched away with the finger tip or a tissue before it dries. Cellulose thinners are used to dilute the lacquer, the type to use is usually recommended by the manufacturer of the lacquer.

Before any lacquering can commence the items have to be perfectly clean and free from grease. Hot water and detergent cannot be used as they discolour copper. The thinner used for diluting the lacquer is one of the best solvents and can be used several times before it becomes too contaminated to clean effectively. There is also a cheaper variety available used for cleaning spray guns.

The fumes given off by cellulose products are highly flammable and even explosive in the right circumstances so you should ensure that there is plenty of ventilation when they are being used and certainly no naked flames or sparking

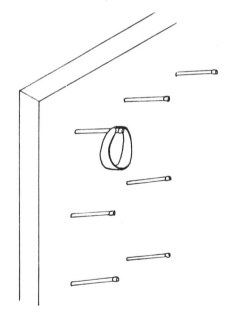

14   Method of suspending copper rings to dry after lacquering

machinery in the vicinity. It would be safest to use them in the open air but lacquer is easily damaged by any trace of damp in the air which causes it to turn a milky white, and of course dust will stick to it and spoil the finish. If you ever come within the domain of the Factory Acts there is a whole list of regulations to comply with regarding the use and storage of cellulose solutions.

Rows of nails on a wooden board are ideal for suspending the articles while the lacquer dries. If driven in at an angle as shown in fig. 14 there is the minimum of contact between the nail and the article and only the tiniest blemish remains when the lacquer has dried. If the nails can be fitted inside a dust free ventilated cupboard so much the better. The drying process can be accelerated by the installation of a 100 watt bulb at the base of the cupboard in which case there must be inlet holes at the bottom and outlet holes at the top so that the warm air will drive any fumes upwards and out through the ventilation holes at the top. A muslin filter over the inlet holes will prevent any dust being circulated along with the air. The heat will also help to remove any traces of damp from the air.

If the articles do become contaminated by damp lacquer begins to show as a milky bloom at the edges and corners. If it is only slight it can sometimes be eradicated by holding the items, one or two at a time in front of an electric fire. If this does not work the only solution is to soak them in thinners to remove the lacquer and relacquer them.

The large sheets of copper that the non-ferrous metal dealer stocks appear to have a beautiful shine but when you examine them closely you will probably find a 'grain' left by the rolling mill and a few scratches where the sheets have been slid together and specks of grit have been dragged across the surface. If these are visible on your piece of jewellery they will have to be polished out. It will require an initial polish on a stitched calico mop using tripoli compound to remove them, followed by a finishing polish on a reflex or swansdown mop using rouge.

Usually any patterns are applied after the initial polish because this is so fierce it would take the edge off these and give a slightly worn appearance. Also oxidizing is done after bending and cleaning has taken place then any highlights polished in on the finishing mop.

All traces of tripoli will have to be washed away with thinners before the finishing polish is applied otherwise traces of tripoli will contaminate the finishing mop and prevent it giving a fine polish.

Applying the copper to the calico mop will generate a fair amount of heat and it may be found necessary to rest the copper on a block of wood or a piece of leather otherwise the heat will build up sufficiently to burn the fingers and cause you to release it.

It is not necessary to put a finish polish on the inside of rings

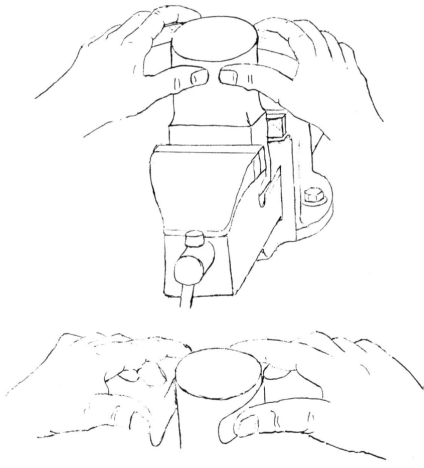

15   Bending a copper bracelet round a wooden former

and bangles or on the back of earrings and pendants. After the initial polish rings and bangles can be bent into shape then cleaned before being given the final polish on the outside only.

The bending operation is quite simple, the bangles can be shaped around a suitably shaped piece of timber clamped in the vice. It will have to be slightly thinner than the average wrist to allow for the springiness in the metal. It is first bent around the wood as shown in figs. 15A and B then finished off with a mallet as shown in fig. 16. The cleaning is carried out after the bending because, as you can see, the copper will end up with a fair number of finger marks over it.

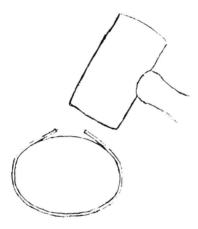

16   Finishing off the ends of the bracelet

Rings are bent around a piece of ⅝'' (15mm) diameter piece of dowel held in the vice. The operation is the same as before and a mallet used to tap the ends into place.

2 Speeding up Production

Most of the processes so far described can be speeded up considerably. The metal merchant who supplies the copper sheet will usually have a large guillotine on the premises and for a small charge will slice a large sheet into strips. If you make the strips 6½'' wide, the length of a bracelet, these can then be sliced into strips for bracelets and rings.

A bench guillotine cuts much quicker and cleaner than tin shears and puts a lot less strain on the hands but one with blades long enough to take a 6½'' bite in a single operation is something of a monster to fit into the average jeweller's workshop as it is built sufficiently robust to chomp into thick steel sheet. A smaller, more conveniently sized machine will do the job in two bites but you will end up with a kink where the two cuts join and it is very difficult to remove them. Also you will have the tedious job of scribing lines on the copper to mark where the cuts go and then trying to keep to them while making the cut.

Fig. 17 shows a simple, home made device for cutting continuously. Once the cutting wheels are set in the required position all the strips will be of identical width without the need to scribe any lines. The only items you may have to buy are a pair of matching gear wheels, everything else can be made from scrap or stock material. A firm supplying spare parts for power tools is a likely place to obtain the gear wheels. Failing that a scrap motor car dealer may be able to help, as some of the older windscreen wiper motors had hardened steel gear wheels in them of the right diameter. They should be of a diameter that allows cutting rollers of between 3 and 4cm in diameter to be used. Smaller than that and the machining of the parts becomes too fiddly and too much effort is needed to

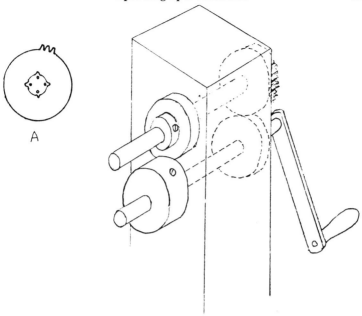

A

17   Machine for slicing sheet into strips. 'A' shows how gear is
secured to shaft

force the copper sheet into the rollers. Larger than that and
everything else, including the machining, becomes magnified
in proportion.

It is important that the two holes carrying the shafts be
drilled undersize and brought up to the correct size with a
reamer and silver steel (unhardened) be used for the shafts.
This way you can be sure of getting a perfect fit. Twist drills
even when new tend to drill slightly oversize which would
result in side play in the shafts which in turn would allow the
cutting wheels to be forced apart by the copper and become
jammed.

There are three ways of securing the gear wheels to the
shaft. Squaring the ends of the shafts and making a matching
square hole in the gears is the most positive and the least likely
to be effected by wear but takes a lot of tedious work with files
to get a good fit. The other two methods are much quicker and
almost as fault proof. If the gears are made of hardened steel
however you will be unable to work on them with anything

other than a grindstone in which case the shaft ends will have to be made a tight interference fit in the gears assisted by a spot of super glue. This grip can also be improved by grinding four notches in the hole in the gears in the positions shown at 17A then, with a centre punch, forcing a piece of the metal of the shaft into the notches.

The upper cutting wheel should be as narrow as the narrowest strip you wish to cut. It will reduce friction between the wheel and the body of the machine if you make it .5mm thinner and fill the gap with a .5mm thick washer.

The cutting wheels are made from silver steel. These too should be drilled undersize then reamered to the right size. Do not forget to drill and tap the grub screw holes before the wheels are hardened and tempered.

The cutting wheels will be a more secure fit on the shafts if you can decide beforehand what widths of strip you will be needing then drill a small hole in the shaft at that setting and turn the end of the grub screw to fit the hole. The grub screw will be less likely to break under the considerable strain put on it if that too is made from silver steel and hardened and tempered.

The cutting wheels should not overlap by more than 1mm. The more they overlap the broader is the cutting angle they present to the copper and the more force needed to push the copper through them. At 1mm hardly any force should be needed and the cutting action smooth and fast. A hundred lengths can be sliced off in a matter of minutes with hardly any distortion of the edges.

The handle will need to have a square hole at the end and a matching square filed on the end of the shaft to take it. It is secured in place with a retaining screw and washer threaded into the end of the shaft. To reduce wear and tear on the fingers the handgrip should be free to rotate in its hole or a loose brass sleeve fitted over it.

Depending on the size of the mild steel bar used for the body of the machine you may find difficulty in keeping the copper sheet at right angles to the cutting wheels. If this is so a piece of angle iron bolted to the body as shown in fig. 18 will provide a larger area for the copper to bear against and maintain an accurate cut.

The bracelet lengths drop from the machine curled up in a

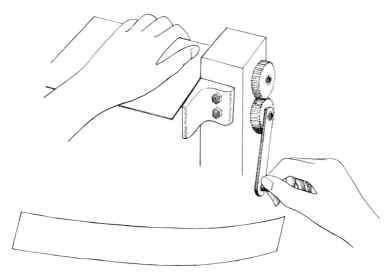

18   Sheet slicing machine in use

circle. They are opened up roughly by hand then passed through the rolling mill making sure that the rollers are spotlessly clean before doing so. Initially tighten the rollers down on to the strip so that it is just gripped by them then remove the strip and close the rollers down a minute fraction. When the copper strip is passed through them it should come out smooth and flat but not elongated more than a couple of millimeters. If there are any deep scratches on any of the strips they should be polished out with emery paper first then the action of the rollers will usually finish the job and remove any remaining marks.

To speed up the process of rounding up the ends and ensuring that they are all uniform a punch and die as in fig. 19 is needed. The base plate is a piece of mild steel sheet about 5mm thick and large enough to span the hole in the base of the fly press. The cutting part of the die is a disc of silver steel about 5mm thick and of a diameter to suit the width of the bracelet being trimmed. If it is made circular as in the illustration and the centre drilled accurately it can be rotated to a new area as the edge becomes dulled with use. The best way to ensure that the hole is centred accurately is to drill it in the lathe after the diameter has been turned to size. It should

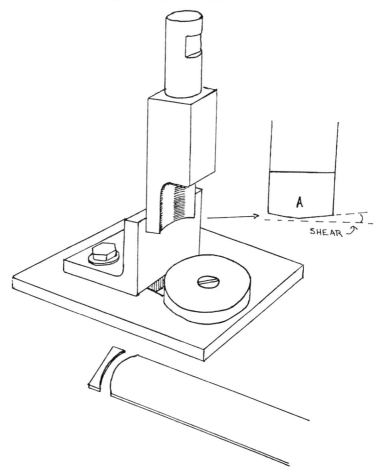

19   Punch and die for trimming the ends of the bracelets. Showing
at 'A' how shear is applied to the punch

be started with a centre drill first because they are more rigid
than a twist drill and will not tend to wander as a twist drill
will sometimes do. Again, for accuracy, drill the hole
undersize and bring it to size with a reamer held in the tail
stock and rotate the disc by hand. Chamfer the hole with the
centre drill because the retaining screw will have to be flush
with the surface of the disc to avoid scratching the copper
strip. Do not be tempted to use a ready-made screw because

they are not accurate enough. It is a simple job to turn one up with a plain section beneath the head that perfectly fits the hole in the disc. If this is also made from silver steel and hardened and tempered it will last indefinitely and the screwdriver slot will not become distorted with use and leave a raised jagged edge that will scratch the copper.

If the disc is to be turned from a piece of round bar it will not hurt to repeat what will be found in most books on lathe work: silver steel is very tough and a large diameter like that will put a heavy load on a parting-off tool. To reduce this load, and to prevent a chip jamming between the tool and the side of the slot being cut and snapping the tool, it is best to cut two or even three slots side by side and overlapping slightly, advancing each one a little at a time and using plenty of cutting oil. You may end up with steps on the rear of the piece being parted off but this can be turned smooth afterwards.

The piece of mild steel angle adjacent to the disc is a rear support for the punch to prevent it springing away from the disc when in use and leaving a burr on the end of the bracelet. It will need to be very firmly secured with two set screws because you may find it necessary to elongate the holes in

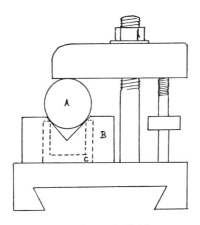

A - ROUND BAR
B - VEE BLOCK
C - CHANNEL

20   Showing how round bar can be gripped in the tool post for
machining

order to get the angle plate to bear accurately against the rear of the punch.

The punch is made from a piece of round or square silver steel rod, round is more readily available but square is easier to grip in the tool post of the lathe. If round has to be used it will be necessary to machine a flat on the back to bear against the angle piece just mentioned and to ensure that it does not move while being machined it will have to be supported on a 'V' block or piece of steel with a slot in it as shown in fig. 20.

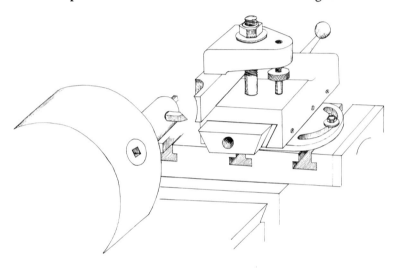

21   Lathe set up for forming the punch to trim bracelet ends

The set up is shown in fig. 21. The boring bar being held in the three-jaw chuck can be any piece of mild steel of sufficient diameter with a hole drilled to take the high speed steel cutter and a tapped hole in the end to take a clamping screw to secure the cutter. Remove the balk of the waste material with a hacksaw first, then set the cutter by eye as close to the correct diameter as possible then check the cut it makes against the edge of the disc. The diameter should either be spot on or slightly under. If it is slightly under you can bring it to the final fit after the balk of the material has been removed.

The base of the punch should finish in a small radius to give it strength and to avoid cracking when it is being hardened. Sharp concave corners should always be avoided where possible on steel that is to be hardened. It is not necessary to harden and temper the whole piece, just the narrow cutting portion.

To save on silver steel, machining, and to make hardening and tempering easier the cutting portion of the punch can be made from a strip of silver steel, hardened and tempered, then bolted to the body of the punch. The body of the punch can then be made out of mild steel. The bolts will have to be positioned so they do not interfere with the back support or be countersunk below the surface. The only disadvantage to making the punch in this manner is the possibility of the bolts working loose with the vibration, a coating of superglue on the mating surfaces will reduce that risk.

The width of the punch should be wider than the bracelet so the ends can be snipped off quickly without the need for accurate alignment.

It should not require much power to chomp off the ends with this device and the power needed can always be reduced by putting shear on the punch which merely means grinding the face of the punch to a slight angle as shown at 'A' in fig. 19. This makes it cut like shears: a little at a time rather than all in one go. There are many occasions when shear can be put on a punch often allowing you to stamp out a blank that would otherwise be completely out of the scope of your press. Remove only the smallest amount to begin with, then try it. Increase the angle of the shear until it will cut easily without

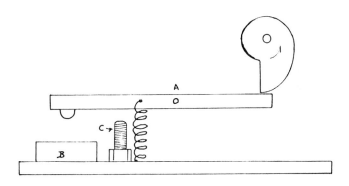

A – Pivot.   B – Anvil.   C – Depth Stop

22   Motor driven planishing device

distorting the copper bracelet. If there is any burr left on the end of the bracelet it may be that the punch is springing away from the die in which case the bolt holes will have to be elongated as mentioned earlier so that the punch support can be positioned accurately. Once it is working properly a hole can be drilled between the two bolts and a tight fitting steel pin driven into the hole to prevent any further movement.

Planishing. A simple electric motor-driven machine for planishing is shown in fig. 22. It consists of a spring loaded arm on a central pivot operated by a cam driven by an electric motor. The speed of the motor will have to be reduced by a four to one ratio of pulleys if it is a standard induction motor running at approximately 1500 rpm so that the hammer strikes about five blows per second. It is quite simple to construct because no great accuracy is required. The size and power of the spring will govern the size and layout of the machine and a certain amount of experiment will be required to get it working properly. To this end it will be necessary to make several holes at different positions on the hammer arm so that the spring can be tried at different positions. Also the radius of the hammer will influence things to a certain extent; obviously it will require less power to make an indentation with a small radius than it will with a large one so in that case the spring would need to be anchored nearer to the hammer where it has less leverage. If it is found that the indentations are too deep at the weakest setting of the spring a depth stop shown at 'c' can be fitted. It is just an ordinary nut and bolt screwed into the base. When the height has been set the bolt is locked in position by tightening the nut against the base.

The machine has the advantage that differently shaped anvils can allow concave or convex shapes to be planished. The big disadvantage is the noise it makes; it is no greater than the noise created when doing it by hand but it is far more rapid and even and tends to get on the nerves. Mounting it on fibre board with a piece of rubber carpet underlay in between reduces the sound and surrounding it on three sides with sound-absorbing material helps to stop the neighbours complaining.

A more simple and silent, though less versatile, method is to put the pattern on a roller and fit it into the rolling mill. A small rolling mill with rollers about 5cm wide and of similar or smaller diameter is ideal for this purpose because the upper roller can usually be removed quite quickly by slackening off the bearings. Also the bearing screws are adjusted individually so it is possible to get the pattern even across the width of the roller. With a set of rollers like those illustrated on page 14, fig. 2, having extensions for pattern rollers there is a limit to how wide a strip you can pattern because of the springiness of the steel extension that carries the rollers. Though a short stub of 3cm diameter could hardly be considered as springy it only takes the minutest difference in pressure, side to side, to make the pattern appear uneven and for the strip to take on a distinct outward curve. A look at the ready-made pattern rollers available from the manufacturer will give you an idea of the limitations as to width.

With the small rolling mill mentioned earlier it is in theory possible to use the whole width of the roller but as they are usually operated without the help of reduction gears it would be extremely tiring and as the widest of bracelets seldom exceeds 3cm it would be a waste of time and energy.

Making a spare roller is a very simple matter. If you buy a piece of mild steel bar of the right diameter and length from the steel merchant, then it is just a matter of mounting it in the lathe, turning down the journals and cutting a 3cm wide groove for the pattern. The depth of the groove will be decided by the thickness of the copper sheet used. If 1.5mm thick sheet is used, which is the ideal thickness for bracelets, then the groove would need to be 1.25mm deep leaving .25mm for the depth of the pattern. This may not seem much for the depth of the pattern but in actual fact you may find that this is too much. It is quite surprising how shallow an indentation is needed to create a very clear pattern; you only have to look at the lettering on a coin to realize this.

If the original roller has a square formed on the end to take the handle then it is just a matter of filing a similar square on your new roller, then you are ready to apply the pattern. If, however, the handle is held in place by a keyway you may think that this is beyond your capabilities or the scope of your lathe; this is not the case. Though the original was probably formed on a milling or shaping machine a keyway can be cut very easily on a lathe. First a round hole, the width and depth of the keyway, is drilled where the keyway is to end. A parting tool the same width or narrower than the keyway is mounted sideways in the tool post. The headstock should be prevented from rotating by using the back gears or a clamp. The parting tool is moved to where the keyway commences then brought to bear against the metal then it is moved along the track of the keyway by traversing the carriage. The tool will peel off a small shaving that will end when it reaches the hole you have drilled. You just repeat this process until the keyway is deep enough. If your lathe is not robust enough, or your parting tool not wide enough to do the cut in one go, just make another overlapping cut until the keyway is the right width. Internal keyways are cut in a similar manner using a boring bar mounted in the toolpost with a suitable cutter in place of the parting tool.

It only remains to apply the pattern: this is done with a hammer and a hardened punch. Experiment first on a piece of flat steel to find the right diameter and curve for the tip of the punch. The curve should be the absolute minimum to get a clear definition; if you make it deeper than necessary you may find unsightly flats on the highlights of the resulting pattern on the copper. Practise a little so you know exactly how hard to hit the punch to achieve this depth. When you are confident you have got it right apply the pattern to the roller.

Of course the pattern on the copper will be the reverse of planishing but it is as equally attractive. The roller can be used in the unhardened state but it will last far longer if it is case hardened. There are many firms specializing in the heat treatment of metals and the charge for case hardening the roller would be quite modest so it is hardly worth while tackling this tricky process yourself.

From what has been described so far it will be obvious that you need not limit yourself to a simple planishing pattern. Using different shaped punches or dental burrs it is possible to create a whole range of patterns and designs and mild steel is a relatively easy material to engrave if you are handy with a graver. Cutting a continuous line on a convex surface is not so easy but a series of short digs to form a continuous line is quite easy and though it looks a bit amateurish on the roller the reverse image on the copper does not.

Some difficulty may be experienced in keeping the copper

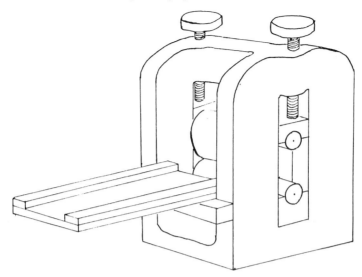

23 Strip guide for use when rolling patterns

strip in line with and central to the rollers. It is not possible to guide it with your hands as the sharp edges will cut into your fingers with the pressure needed to guide the strip. A steel guide along the lines shown in fig. 23 will be necessary.

It is made up of stock sizes of mild steel strip. The crosspiece enables you to get a firm grip on it and brace it against the uprights of the rolling mill. Alternatively a couple of holes can be drilled and tapped into the uprights and the crosspiece bolted to it. The top of the guide is left open to enable you to force out any pieces that become jammed in the guide; if the top is covered you have to take the whole thing to pieces to free it.

Considerable stretching will occur when the copper is passed through the rollers and some experimentation will be necessary to calculate the length of copper required to produce a bracelet length. If all your copper is precut to 6.5″ as suggested earlier the excess length will have to be trimmed off. But the pieces need not be wasted as they can be used to make small earrings or ring blanks.

The supplementary rollers that fit on to extensions on some rolling mills can obviously be used for the same purpose though, as mentioned earlier, you are limited to the width of these rollers. You will not have to make the blank roller yourself in this case because the firms that supply patterned rollers for these mills will also supply you with an annealed blank. One drawback is that the steel they use even in its annealed state is considerably harder than mild steel and can usually only be worked with diamond tipped burrs. But a large round burr will make the same impression as a punch, it just takes longer.

A guide similar to the one described can be used for this type of roller, the only difference being that it can be supported on one side only but if the crosspiece is sufficiently robust it will work just as well.

All this may seem like a lot of tedious and difficult work but a complete roller should not take more than two days to make from start to finish and if hardened will last indefinitely. And if the punches you use are well polished the finish will be transferred to the roller and then to the copper so that very little finish polishing will be required. You can then produce with one turn of the handle a bracelet that would take perhaps half an hour of handwork so that the time spent making the roller will very soon be regained and it is all profit from there on.

Another device that may seem like a lot of hard work to begin with, but which can pay for itself over and over again, is illustrated at fig. 24.

It is a miniature rolling mill in effect but only used for applying a pattern along the edge of a wide bracelet or down the centre of a narrow one. Its distinct advantage is in the smallness of the pattern wheels. A new one can be designed, made, and be working within an hour or two.

The dimensions of the machine are not shown because they will depend on the size of the matching pair of gears. As in the case of the slicing machine they should ideally be between 20 and 25mm in diameter, but also with teeth that are deep enough to allow them to be moved apart by about one mm without disengaging. This is to allow the depth of the pattern to be varied and different thicknesses of metal to be patterned.

With gears of 20 to 25mm diameter the two lengths of brass 'U' channel should be about 12cm long to give sufficient leverage for the pressure adjusting screw 'B'. A gap of 3mm between the two channels will be sufficient to allow for the

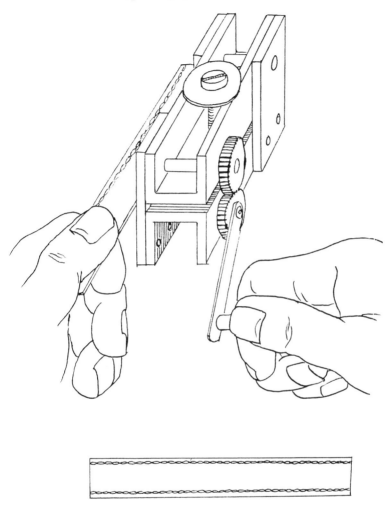

24   Pattern rolling machine in use

pressure adjustment. Brass is used because it is readily obtainable in this form, is easy to machine and sufficiently rigid and
hardwearing. The three uprights are also of brass for the same
reasons, but mild steel could be used if it happens to be on
hand. The pivot bar and the shafts for the gears are unhardened
silver steel. The pivot bar is just a push fit into the holes; it is
subjected to very little movement so will stay in place.

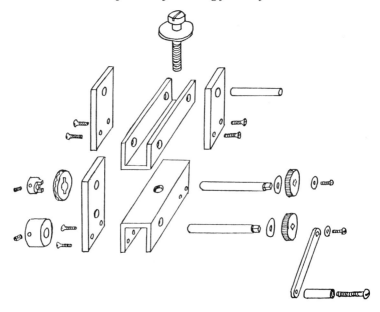

25   Pattern rolling machine, exploded view

The adjusting screw passes through the upper arm and screws into the lower arm. If a short length of square steel bar is fitted securely into the lower arm this can be used to clamp the machine in the vice when in use.

If only two or three pattern rollers are to be made it is best to turn short shoulders on them to take the grub screw but if more than that are contemplated it is best to make the short collar 'G' with two prongs to fit into matching slots in the wheels. This way the wheels are quicker and easier to make and there is no collar to obstruct the file when forming the pattern.

The upright next to the pattern wheel is necessary to keep the bracelet lined up with the wheel and stop it slipping into the gap between the two arms. The upper hole through which the shaft passes should be elongated slightly to allow the upper arm to move up and down when the pressure is being adjusted. The lower roller should be wide enough to allow the grub screw hole to clear the bracelet and should be polished but not necessarily hardened.

In use the pressure screw is slackened off and the desired

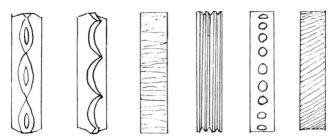

26   Some samples of pattern rollers

wheel clamped into position. A piece of scrap copper the same thickness as the bracelet to be patterned is placed between the rollers and the pressure screw tightened until the depth of the pattern is right then the bracelet is passed through the rollers. Keep the two shafts well oiled to ease the operation and prolong the life of the machine.

Fig. 26 shows a sample of rollers that are easily shaped up with needle files. No. 3 is a plain roller with random file marks around it. No. 5 is a plain roller with shallow holes drilled around it and No. 6 is a plain roller with diagonal file marks. Though they may appear unimpressive the three dimensional effect when they are rolled into the copper is very attractive.

The holes to take the prongs of the fixing collar are cut out roughly with a piercing saw, or drilled, then finished off to a sliding fit with a three cornered needle file. When they have been hardened they should be cleaned up with fine emery paper, then tempered by heating from the central hole and quenched when the pattern is pale yellow.

Punched Patterns. Though an infinite number of patterns and designs can be built up from a variety of small punches every punch mark has to be applied individually and this is very time consuming. It is possible to put a fairly large design on a large punch using needle files, dental burrs and small punches but the larger the design the heavier the blow needed, even using a two-pound hammer. The result is that it is difficult to keep the punch correctly lined up and vertical while swinging a heavy hammer with the other hand. To overcome this problem the simple punch guide illustrated in fig. 27 is a real boon. It is made from mild steel bar and drilled and bolted

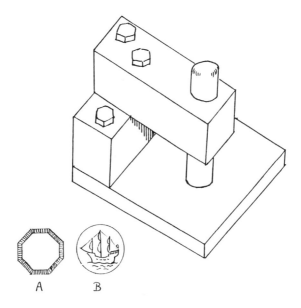

27   Home made punch guide

together but unless it is tack welded as well the vibration caused by the constant hammering will soon loosen the bolts. It will need to be used on a very heavy metal support and preferably bolted down. A short section of steel joist is ideal for this purpose.

A 12mm diameter punch is about the limit with this method using a two-pound hammer but a lot depends on the type of pattern to be impressed. A border pattern as in 'A' fig. 27, where the shaded parts are cut away leaving only the plain areas to be impressed on the copper would require only a light blow whereas 'B', where only the lines have been cut away with a graver leaving a much larger plain area would require quite a heavy blow.

Small punches can be fitted into the fly press enabling a repetitive pattern to be applied quite easily but it would require a much heavier press (No. 4 or 5) than the one illustrated to get a satisfactory impression from a 12mm diameter punch. This would take up a great deal more space than the hammer guide. In addition the punches would have to have a wide collar turned on them to spread the pressure of the blow on the face of the slide or else the hole in the slide would eventually become distorted by the constant hammering.

Punches for use in the guide can be cut from round silver steel bar and hardened and tempered quite easily with a propane torch used on a bed of charcoal or fire brick.

The pattern on the head of the punches can be quite shallow and still produce a very visible impression. All the smooth areas should be finished with fine emery paper and repolished after hardening and tempering as any file marks or bits of scale will reproduce quite clearly on the copper. The tail of the punch should be rounded as shown to ensure that the blow is delivered to the centre of the punch giving an even impression.

If the pattern is cut into a disc of silver steel and then bolted to the base plate of the guide and a blank punch used to force the copper into it a stronger, three dimensional effect can be obtained.

Using this method it is not too difficult using gravers and burrs to cut a set of simplified zodiac signs like those illustrated on page 168. If the area of the disc to be patterned is slightly hollowed out and the punch domed to match the three dimensional effect is more striking.

Obviously the same punch is used for all twelve discs and if cutting twelve discs seems like a lot of work remember that they can be used for rings, earrings, charms and small pendants as well and the popularity of the zodiac signs never seems to dwindle. Unlike casting and long run production methods you do not have to carry large reserve stocks to cater for the extra demand of one particular sign: it takes only a matter of minutes to clamp the disc into the punch guide and bang out a few extras.

Drop Hammer. One other method of delivering a heavy blow to a small area is by using a drop hammer. One version of this machine is illustrated in fig. 28. It consists of a very heavy cast-iron base surmounted by two iron guide rails. The hammer, a cast-iron block with a hardened face, is free to slide up and down between the rails. A rope and pulley is used to haul the hammer to the top of the rails. These machines have largely been replaced by power presses and hydraulic presses

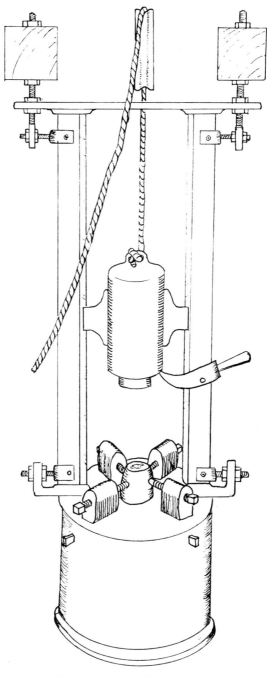

28   One type of drop hammer

but as they are virtually indestructible and ideal for short-run work there are still a few lurking around in second-hand machinery merchants' warehouses.

They must have been around for quite some time because a Mr Nasmyth invented a steam driven version in 1839, a model of which can be seen in the Science Museum. Prior to that there is in existence a model built from a design by Leonardo da Vinci. This was intended to be used for cutting out coin blanks from strip material and is operated by two capstans, but the basic principle is there: a heavy weight sliding vertically between two guide bars. He said of it, 'This cuts coins of perfect roundness, thickness and weight, and saves the need of the man who makes the coins round. They pass therefore merely through the hands of the worker of the plate and the stamper, and they are very fine coins.' It is something of a puzzle why a man of Leonardo's genius did not see that this machine could also replace the man with the hammer. At any rate he must have been way ahead of his time again or his notes lost because when screw operated coining machines were adopted a century later they were still cutting and shaping the blanks by hand. An engraving in Diderot's *Encyclopedia of the Sciences* (1751) shows a huge coining press with an operating arm about four metres long with a huge iron ball on each end. There are ropes attached to the balls and four people needed to haul on the ropes. Again one wonders why such a complicated engineering project was used – imagine cutting a matching thread 20cm in diameter by hand – when a large weight falling between guides would have done the job.

In the more recent past they were used a lot for making military badges and medals. Jewellers used them for forming items that required more power than the average screw press could deliver.

They are in effect a giant sized version of the hammer and punch guide just described. The dies are usually cone shaped blocks of steel; this shape allows them to be firmly held in position and hard against the base by the four clamping screws. A softened metal blank is placed on the die and the hammer raised. As the hammer is lifted the retaining claw is pulled aside by the weight of its handle. The hammer is released and falls on the blank forcing it into whatever shape is cut into the die. As the hammer bounces back up the guides the retaining claw is flipped back into place and holds the hammer while the formed blank is removed and another put in its place.

It is ideal for making St Christopher medals, imitation coins, bracelet links or pendants. It takes time to make the dies but once made and properly hardened they will last indefinitely. A small order for fifty or so of these items could be completed in two or three hours whereas to cast them, which is the only alternative, would take at least two days.

The St Christopher die in the illustration, fig. 29, is an extra large one intended for mounting on a magnet so it can be stuck on a car dashboard. It was made from an old redundant die which had been softened and the head cleaned off on the lathe. The outline circle was cut while it was still mounted in the lathe using a shallow 'V' shaped tool. The remainder of the engraving was done with ordinary round HSS burrs in the pendant drill. The waves were cut with a sharp edged burr. An ordinary square graver was used for the hair and eyelids. From start to finish it took a little over three hours, the hardening being done by a specialist.

It was first given a coating of engineers blue and the figures roughly marked out with a scriber. The staff was cut initially using a 1mm round burr and with the same burr all the

29   St Christopher die for use in drop hammer

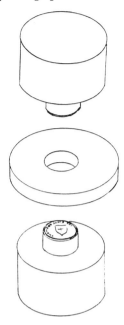

30 Medal die used in a drop hammer

outlines were shallowly marked. A plasticine impression is then taken to see if all the proportions are right. A larger burr is then used to indent the deeper areas: head, arms, legs and folds of cloths. If another impression shows that things are going right the finer details are cut using progressively smaller burrs until the final finishing touches with the graver.

The two smaller dies with the circular object between them in fig. 30 are a pair of medal dies and their retaining ring. These are used to create a small double sided jubilee medal. As with most medals and coins they are thicker at the edge than in the centre. This is done by turning a small recess round the edge of both upper and lower die. The retaining ring is hardened and tempered steel, with the hole an accurate sliding fit over the projections on the dies. In use the lower die is clamped to the base of the drop hammer, the retaining ring placed over it. A close-fitting, softened blank is put into the hole and the upper die slid in after it. When the hammer is dropped on to it, in addition to impressing the design on to both faces of the medal it also forces the metal into the recesses round the circumference. A milled edge can be applied to the medal by filing lines on the inside of the hole in the retaining ring. The lines have to be made perfectly perpendicular or the medal will be very difficult to remove from the ring. A smear of oil to the inside of the ring will make removal a little easier but will not compensate for inaccurate lines.

Although a skilled engraver could carve the reverse lettering seen on the dies, they could be cut on an engraving machine using a specially made template. They could also be done using letter punches like those shown in fig. 30A. You do not need to make a whole alphabet in one go, just enough to complete the first job then they can be added to as the need arises. They are easily shaped by needle files on silver steel rod and the inside of the 'O's and 'B's etc cut with round burrs and the sharp corners picked out with a graver. When hardened and tempered an impression from the punch is made in a heavy strip of silver steel. When the alphabet is complete or the strip of steel is full it is then hardened and tempered and is used to form the head on any future punches should any become worn or broken. The block that the punches in the illustration are resting on is one of these. A blank punch is made and while still soft the point is hammered into the appropriate letter. After trimming off any burrs it then only needs to be hardened and tempered.

Some drop hammers have heavy shock absorbing springs built into the base and this type can be surface mounted on a concrete floor. On the one shown in the illustration there are no shock absorbers, instead the base has an additional piece

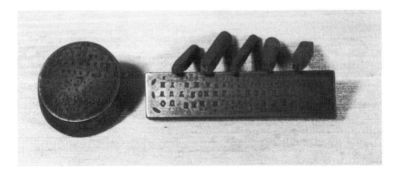

30a   Letter punches

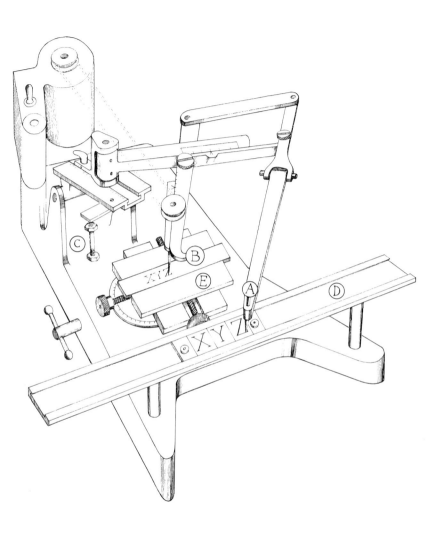

31   Engraving machine with added depth stop at 'C'

half as long again and spreading out dovetail fashion and this piece is set into a concrete platform wide and deep enough to prevent the constant hammering driving the anvil into the ground.

Engraving. The machine has not yet been invented that can imitate good hand engraving but there are machines on the market capable of engraving attractive designs on jewellery. It can be done with a burr fitted in the pendant drill but it is difficult to control and is a relatively slow process. The same can be said of the vibration type machines which are hand held and used like a pen and rely on a sharp vibrating point to trace out the design freehand.

The pantograph engraving machine however holds out greater possibilities. Though the larger machines would have to be used a great deal to justify the outlay, a small secondhand one can be made to do a variety of work and would not break the bank.

The illustration fig. 31 is one that is designed mainly for engraving small flat name plates though it is capable of engraving on slightly concave or convex surfaces. It uses either a rotating steel cutter to carve the lines or a non-rotating diamond point to gouge the lines. On copper it would only be practical to use the diamond point because, as mentioned earlier, copper is a 'sticky' material to machine and the resulting lines would be burred and a little ragged.

The machine is divided into three main components: the vice 'E', the pantograph frame carrying the stylus 'A' and the cutting tool, and the worktable 'D'. The vice can be moved horizontally or vertically in the same plane and rotated through 360 degrees. The engraving is always reduced in size to the pattern, the degree of reduction controlled by the position of the two scales on the pantograph arms.

In use the stylus 'A' is controlled by the right hand and the cutter raised and lowered by the left hand holding the knob 'B'.

Alphabet templates in various styles of lettering can be purchased which have top and bottom edges bevelled to fit the bevelled grooves in the worktable. They are slid in from the ends of the worktable and kept in position moveable by screw stops at each end. They are indispensible for one-off lettering jobs but for repetition work be it lettering or patterns it is more practical to make your own composite template. This is done by drawing or tracing the design roughly four times oversize on to a piece of stiff card or plywood; this is then clamped to the worktable with 'G' clamps and a piece of brass or acrylic sheet clamped in the vice. The lines of the design are carefully followed with the stylus while the rotating cutter duplicates it on the material in the vice. The reduction will eliminate most of the inaccuracies caused by an unsteady hand while any remaining can be corrected with a burr or graver. The engraving is then placed on the worktable and used as the pattern. The design will again be reduced when it is re-engraved on the new workpiece so that any remaining inaccuracies will vanish.

If markers or a jig are fitted to the vice so that the workpiece can be placed in position quickly and accurately a fair speed of production can be reached.

Examples of such templates or patterns are shown in fig. 31a. The first two on the top row are small pendants or charms: the shamrock leaves were intended to be recessed with the engraving tool and the recesses filled with enamel. The third, a good luck charm, will be discussed later. The coat

31a   Templates and patterns

of arms on the bottom row had to be reduced several times to fit on a small commemorative medal which had too short a run to justify a die as with the one on the bottom right. The latter was for a badge ordered by the landlord of a pub who had a spate of his customers falling off the bar stools so he declared that this qualified them for membership of the Commercial Club and they received a lapel badge, or in the ladies case a pendant with the same design. It smoothed ruffled feathers and stopped them blaming his unstable bar stools.

This multiple reduction method can be used for cutting a design into the head of a punch. If there is no play in the pantograph a surprising amount of intricate detail can be placed on a very small punch.

The depth to which the engraving tools cut is controlled by a nose cone fitted over the end of the cutter. It has the disadvantage that you cannot see the point of the cutter which makes it a little difficult to place it accurately; also you are limited to using cutters specifically made for that machine. In the illustration fig. 31 a large bolt 'C' can be seen: this is screwed into the base and there is a locking nut to keep it in place. A bar fitted to the pantograph comes into contact with the head of the bolt when the cutter is lowered to the workpiece. By raising or lowering the bolt the depth of cut can be controlled without the use of the nose cone. This also allows you to use non-standard cutters which can be a considerable saving as the ready-made ones are quite expensive. Most hobby shops stock a range of brass tubes one of which matches the diameter of the cutting tools of this machine and by coincidence the inside diameter of the tube is a perfect match for the shanks of the burrs used in the pendant drill. Consequently any worn or broken burrs receive a new lease of life as engraving tools after being suitably ground and superglued into the end of a length of tube. If the diameters of other makes of engraving machine cutters are different, it is a simple job to turn down a piece of brass bar and drill a hole in the end to take any diameter of cutting material available.

Another modification that can be made to the machine is that special jaws can be made to fit the vice and shapes cut in them to take an awkwardly shaped workpiece. The original jaws are made from tough thermosetting plastic but replacements can be made from plywood or acrylic sheet or almost any material soft enough not to damage the cutter should it accidentally strike them. They are just pressed into place on to two steel pegs so the original jaws can be used as templates to accurately position the holes to take the pegs on your home made jaws.

Copper Rings. Rings whose sides are parallel can be made in exactly the same way as the bracelets as they are only miniature versions of the same thing. Rather than slice them one at a time from a copper strip of the right width as with the bracelets it is more practical and a great deal quicker to cut one long width of ring width, pattern it, then divide it into ring lengths using a double-sided version of the die used to trim the bracelet ends. As with the latter it is better to make it a little oversize, i.e. wider than the width of the rings, so that it is not necessary to place the strip over the die with extreme accuracy. Though guides could be fitted either side of the hole in the die the slightest inaccuracy in the width of the strip would cause it to jam in the guides and with different patterns being applied to the rings it would be impossible to ensure that they were of uniform width because some patterns would spread the metal more than others.

When making a punch and die of this type it is necessary to work out in detail which is the easier part to make first because the part you make first can be used to make the other part. In the present example if it was necessary to make the sharp corners in the hole in the die plate, fig. 32A, it would be nearly impossible to do this even with a very fine piercing saw blade whereas the punch can be made easily and accurately in the lathe in the same way as the bracelet punch or easier still, with this small diameter, by drilling two suitably spaced holes in the head of the punch as shown in fig. 32B, then cutting away the unwanted material.

If the amount of waste is going to be excessive due to the diameter of the holes it is possible to use a piece of silver steel that is just large enough to form the punch then pad it out with two pieces of mild steel as shown, fig. 32c, and clamp it all tightly together while the holes are drilled. With the punch accurately formed and hardened and tempered it can be fitted in the press, and with the hole in the die plate cut as near as possible to the right shape and size but still in the annealed

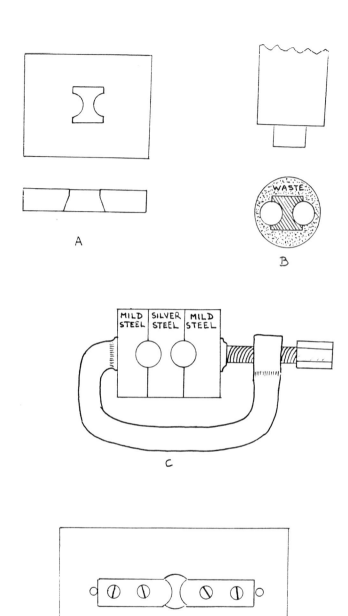

A

B

C

MILD STEEL | SILVER STEEL | MILD STEEL

WASTE

D

32 Punch and die for chopping strip into ring lengths and rounding the ends at the same time

state the punch is lowered over the hole, accurately centred, then given a sharp thump. The punch will only penetrate the die for a very short distance because even in its annealed state silver steel is still extremely tough. If insufficient metal was removed from the die hole the punch may not penetrate at all but just leave an outline of its shape around the hole. This is sufficient for you to work on and will act as a guide when you begin to enlarge the hole further with needle files.

The hole need only be accurate for a very short depth in order to work properly, in this case about 1.5mm, for the rest of the distance the metal will be cut back as shown in fig. 32A. If this is not done the pieces of copper will build up in the hole and jam it solid; this also cuts down the amount of accurate work necessary with the punch and files. Sometimes, depending on the shape of the hole, the tapered part of the hole can be turned out roughly on the lathe so considerably reducing the amount of hand-work necessary.

If the punch did penetrate any distance it will have carved metal away from the walls; this will have built up under the head of the punch bringing it to a halt. It is then necessary to remove this with needle files and burrs, being careful not to touch the part that the punch has cut. It need not be cleaned away completely, just sufficient so that the punch can travel a little further with the next thump. This process is repeated until the punch breaks through into the cut-back portion of the hole. It is quite possible that the punch will jam in the hole it has made and cannot be removed by hand in which case it will be necessary to clamp the die plate on to the bed of the press and free the punch by pulling back on the press handle. To reduce the chance of this happening the punch should be oiled each time it is plunged into the die plate.

When the hole is complete, clamp the plate to the bed of the press and try it out on a piece of scrap copper. If the copper pieces pile up in the hole and jam solid, increase the depth of the cut-back until they fall free; there should not be more than two or three together in the hole at any one time. The more there are the greater is the effort required to stamp out the next piece because the preceding ones have to be forced down. When it is working well harden and temper it. Hardening and tempering often dull the cutting edges of the die with the formation of scale which comes away with the quenching. They can be resharpened by drawing them over a carborundum stone a few times; it is not usually necessary to resort to the power grinder for this purpose. Do not be tempted to use the grinder for convenience because at this stage the faces of your die should be perfectly flat and parallel to each other when mounted in the press and it is very difficult to keep them so with hand-held grinding.

In the present case only the curved sides of the punch and die do any cutting because it is wider than the strip being cut therefore the straight sides can be eliminated from the die plate altogether. This allows a much simpler form of die plate to be used. Illustration, fig. 32D will show what is meant. The base plate is a piece of mild steel with a round hole drilled in it to allow the copper pieces to pass through. The two smaller pieces on top are silver steel, their cutting edges filed to fit into the curves of the punch with the lower two thirds cut back then hardened and tempered.

It may be found necessary to elongate the holes of the fixing screws on one side in order to make the punch a perfect fit between them in which case it will be necessary to fit a peg

33   'A' copper ring blank. 'B' blank bent into shape. 'C' method of removing waste metal from centre of ring blanking die

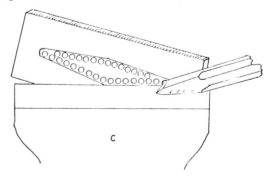

behind the pieces as shown to prevent them being forced apart
again. The peg has to be slightly tapered so it will be a tight fit
in the hole and a spot of superglue in the hole will prevent it
working loose with the vibration.

The tapered sided ring, figs. 33A and B, is an attractive
shape by itself and can be patterned with punches or
engraving; it can also be used as the basis or shank of a ring
with a separate head. The zodiac signs mentioned earlier were
applied to this using the punch guide and sold very well for a
long time.

The punch for making the ring blank is the easier part to
make as the cutting part can be made from a small flat piece of
silver steel and bolted on to a mild steel shank machined to fit
the press. Making the cutting part separate in this way makes
the hardening and tempering a lot easier because of the much
smaller amount of metal to be treated. The silver steel strip
will need to be about 6mm thick to allow shear (see page 42) to
be put on it and also allow the heads of the fixing screws to be
recessed below the surface. The shear will allow a much
smoother and easier cutting action. A flat punch of this size
would require quite a hefty blow to stamp out the blank on a
number two press. The shear also makes the forming of the
die plate easier as it will shave the metal from the insides of the
hole. The slight taper of the shear also tends to guide the
punch into the die which is an advantage should the two parts
happen to move out of alignment. The proof of this is that the
original, due to the lack of a suitable press at the time, was
fitted into the jaws of a number two Record vice and used as a
press for many months. The only modification needed on the
vice was to fit a screw into the side to take up a bit of side play;
the shear coped with the remaining small inaccuracies.

The die plate needs to be 6mm thick to give it sufficient
strength and there should be a minimum distance of 1.5cm
between the closest edge of the hole and the edge of the plate
to eliminate the chance of it cracking under strain. This
sometimes happens with die plates if they are not properly
seated on the press bed due to a speck of grit or fragment of
metal trapped beneath it, so always check that the underside
of the plate and the bed are perfectly clean and the plate does
not rock before putting any pressure on it.

The plate could be made thinner than 6mm if it is mounted

on a slab of mild steel but as most of the hole can be made by drilling there would be no great saving in handwork in this case. If care is taken in spacing the holes so that there is the bare minimum of metal separating them the centre can be easily knocked out with a cold chisel with the plate held in the vice and the hardened jaws used to guide the chisel point, see fig. 33C.

The ideal length for the ring blank is 5.5cm (2.25''). If it is bent around a piece of 1.5cm (⅝'') dowel mounted in the vice in much the same way as the bracelets are formed, the two tails of the ring should just touch. This enables them to be suspended from a nail across the join when they are lacquered so no mark is left when they are dry.

This method of shaping them is so fast that it is hardly worth mechanising the job though there is a machine for shaping flat sheet into cylinders whose principle could be used. The machine is called a slip roll or cylinder bending rollers and consists of three rollers arranged in a triangle formation, fig. 34.

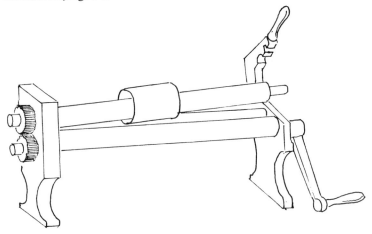

34   Slip rolls or cylinder bending machine.

The front and upper rollers are geared together and can be set so that they grip the metal and feed it through. The rear one can be moved forward or backward and locked in position, this position determines the diameter of the cylinder. The upper roller is usually hinged so that if a complete

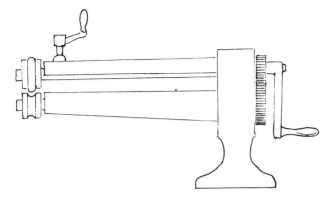

34a   Swage or beading machine

cylinder, rather than just an arc, is formed it can be lifted apart and the cylinder 'slipped' off. Another machine which also normally resides in the sheet-metal workers domain, but of which miniature versions have been found useful in jewellery work, is called a swage, see fig. 34a.

It consists of two arms geared together, the upper one being on a hinge or pivot at the handle end. Various matching pairs of rollers are fitted on the ends and can be used to form a ridge on flat sheet or a bead around a cylinder. The screw above the upper arm controls the depth of the bead. One application in the present text would be to form a convex bangle from flat strip. Any shape of matching rollers could be turned from mild steel bar on the lathe. As they are subjected to very little wear they would not need to be hardened but should you be fortunate enough to gain a large order for one item they could be case hardened.

As mentioned earlier the ring just described can be used as a shank to support a separate head so making it into a dress ring. It could be used as it is with the head soft soldered to it or be given a more finished appearance by having shoulders pressed out of it using the die in fig. 35A. The shoulders are pressed out after the ring blanks have been given their initial polish. When they are bent into shape the shoulders will lift into their correct position. The tips can then be soldered to the head or just bent over it, see Fig. 35B.

The die plate is made first. The two holes 'A' are drilled first

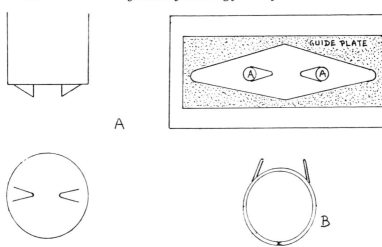

35 'A' Punch for forming shoulders in ring blank. 'B' Die plate with guide and below is the shaped blank with shoulders raised in position

then the 'V's cut out with a piercing saw. The point of the 'V's should be rounded, this reduces the chance of the metal cracking through at the point of the 'V's and makes it easier to harden and temper the punch: a sharp point would get overheated unless great care was taken. The arms of the 'V's in the die plate should be slightly longer than those on the punch so that the punch only cuts the 'V's rather than stamping out a triangle. The face of the punch has shear put on it for the same reason.

Fig. 36 shows four basic shapes that would be suitable for ring heads. On their own they are not very exciting and would entail a considerable amount of work to make the dies so it is worth while giving a bit of thought to alternative uses. The first one 'A' if turned on its side would make a nice bracelet link (see page 88). If two small additional dies were made to produce blanks 'E' and 'F' then A to D could also form earrings if made from thinner material with the centres stamped out as shown at G,H,I,J, and the centres used to embellish the ring heads as shown at K to N. The larger part could be slightly concave and the centre convex and one plain and the other planished to give contrast. In addition, as almost anything can be suspended from a thong or chain and

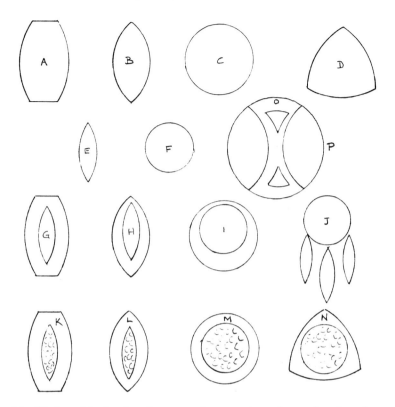

36 Various blanks for rings, pendants and earrings, showing the economical use of dies

called a pendant, the blanks could be so spaced apart that the material between them used as pendants as the example shown at N.

Doming and stamping the blanks can be done at the same time if the punches are slightly domed. There is a limit to how much, because doming the punch in effect blunts it and if overdone will leave a rough edge on the blank which will need to be cleaned up. Or it can be done by hammering them into a hollowed out recess in a piece of hard wood using a matching hard wood punch. Metal doming blocks and punches would be too hard for copper and tend to stretch the metal and spoil any texturing already put on it.

The rings could be assembled in two ways. The first is by

soft soldering them in which case they could be lined up on a fire-brick, head down and heated slightly then a dab of Bakers fluid put at the point of contact and at the points of the shoulders. Then soldered with a very fine strip of solder which would melt quickly on contact before the copper has time to become discoloured.

The other way is by riveting them through the centre with a copper, brass or aluminium rivet the head of which would form part of the decoration. We then come to the problem of making the rivet holes and also the holes in the earrings and pendants to take the connecting rings. Drilling with a twist drill is out because it quickly jams in copper and a drill that fine would easily break. A spade drill assisted by a drop of paraffin for lubrication would work but is just as time consuming. A punch is by far the most efficient method but a punch and die this fine is like taking a sledge hammer to crack a nut.

A pair of punch pliers is one answer. They can sometimes be bought; one variety used to be made for watch and clock work where they were used to punch holes in mainsprings. They usually had three punches arranged one above the other on one jaw of the pliers and a matching plate on the other. They would punch round, square or rectangular holes and are a very handy tool if you can get hold of one. The alternative is to make a pair which is done quite easily by adapting an ordinary pair of flat pliers. Making sure the jaws are soft enough to be drilled, use a twist drill the same diameter as the hole to be punched and drill a hole through both jaws centrally

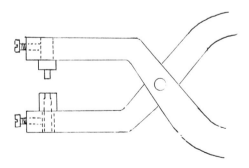

37   Leather worker's crimping pliers used as hole punches for metal

and near the top. Cut off the end cm from the shank of the drill. This is usually soft enough to saw but if not a touch on the grindstone will weaken it so that it can be broken off. This is fitted into one jaw of the pliers and held in place by a clamp screw fitted to the side of the jaw. You might have to fit a depth stop to prevent the jaws closing completely and marking the work piece. A hole drilled and tapped through one handle near the hinge so that when a screw is inserted the end bears against the other handle preventing them being completely closed will serve the purpose.

Ordinary pliers will have a limit to where the hole can be placed depending on the length of the jaws, whereas a pair of leatherworker's crimping pliers will give you much greater scope in this respect but the punch and plate will have to be specially made to fit the holes already in the jaws which take the crimping tools. See fig. 37.

The Pinfold press, fig. 5, could be used for this purpose but the much quicker acting presses figs. 38 and 39 would be more suitable.

The commercially made one in fig. 38 is built more for power than accuracy and principally intended for punching 2 to 5mm rivet holes in mild steel sheet. Its accuracy was improved by the small screw at the front which projects into the slideway and takes up the bit of play but it can still only be

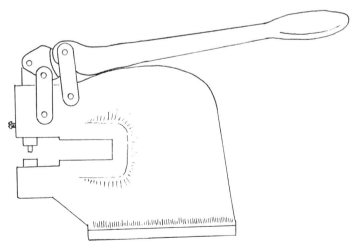

38   Commercially made quick-punch

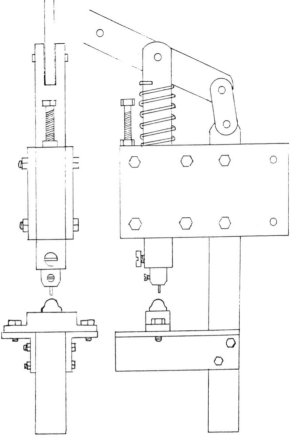

39   Home made quick-punch

used for stamping small round discs.

The second press (fig. 39) was made originally for shaping wedding ring type earrings for which a long stroke and very little power was needed. By altering the position of the bolt holes the leverage was increased enough to enable it to stamp out small shapes and punch fine holes. Though it is simple to make from standard bright mild steel stock it is very accurate as can be seen by the 1mm punch and die fitted. These were made to punch holes in a small hemisphere hence the peculiar shape of the die. A punch of this diameter would be very difficult to harden and temper and is also very fragile. This problem was overcome by making a punch holder in mild steel and using a short length of piano wire – or spring wire as it is sometimes called – coils of which cost very little, clamped into it. If it breaks or becomes blunt you can just throw it away and insert another piece. The press was made to be held in the vice so it could be put out of harms way in a cupboard when not in use.

The jump rings used for looping items together are best made from bronze wire because it is much harder than copper and easier to cut. The rings are formed in quantity by fitting a piece of round rod into the chuck of an ordinary hand brace and clamping it into the vice as shown in fig. 40.

The end of the bronze wire is bent at right angles and the bent portion pushed down between two of the chuck jaws. When the handle is turned the wire will roll onto the rod. The coils have to be kept tightly together and it is advisable to hold the wire in a piece of cloth or leather because quite a bit of heat is generated as it passes through the fingers. The resulting coil will open up slightly when you stop winding enabling it to be slipped off the rod.

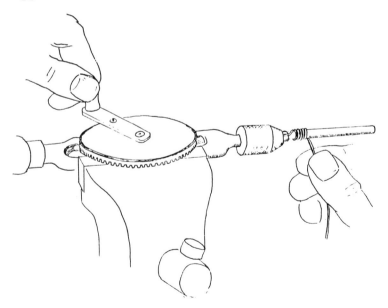

40   Use of hand brace for rolling up jump rings

The same result can be obtained by fitting the rod into the jaws of a chuck in the lathe and the wire wound on using the lowest speed of the lathe. In this case you should wear a pair of protective gloves to hold the wire and so iron out any kinks before it reaches the rod.

Oval links can be made in quantity in the same way taking the usual precaution of winding tissue paper on to the oval rod first and burning it out afterwards to release the coil.

The rings can be cut from the coil in the ordinary way with a piercing saw but if you are making any quantity the machine in fig. 41 will speed up the job and save a lot of saw blades.

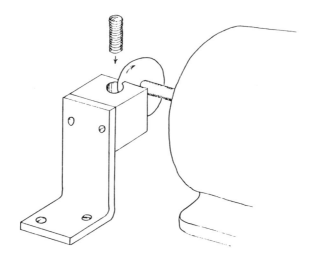

41   Circular saw for sawing off jump rings

The electric motor is an induction or squirrel cage motor running at 1475rpm. The circular saw is an engineer's slitting saw with teeth that are fine enough so that they will not jam on the finest wire to be cut. There is also a circular metal saw used in the device for removing rings from swollen fingers; the circular blades used in this are suitable and obtainable from jewellery tool suppliers. Either of these blades will need to be lubricated with bee's or paraffin wax.

The block with the guide holes can be made from brass or mild steel attached by screws or soldered to a rigid piece of angle iron. Oval rings will pass through a round hole though you may have to guide the coil with a pair of smooth jawed pliers to keep it in line with the blade. The coil should be a sliding fit in the hole and the blade should be set to just cut through the coil and no further. A fairly deep box should be placed beneath the hole to catch the rings because they fly off at quite a speed and will scatter everywhere if not caught. Remember to pickle and clean the rings while they are still on the coil because it is not much fun doing them afterwards one at a time.

Brass. It is obvious that most of the processes described in the previous section could be applied to most metals with a similar malleability to copper. Some varieties of brass fall into this category. Brass is an alloy of copper and zinc in various proportions, the more zinc the less malleable it is but harder and easier to machine. It loses the 'stickiness' of copper and at a certain point becomes what is called free-cutting brass. When this alloy is turned in a lathe or drilled the metal, comes away in a shower of flakes instead of the continuous curled shaving of the lower zinc alloys. The latter are called cartridge brass or deep drawing brass. They are used for forming items in one piece such as cartridge cases – hence the name. Free-cutting brass having a higher zinc content is a paler yellow than cartridge brass which is one way of telling them apart. Another way is to draw a file across the metal: with free-cutting brass the file almost skids across whereas with the other type it tends to dig in. This is a general classification for brasses in common use but there are many other varieties that have additions of other metals for specialist engineering uses.

In deep drawing a circular blank is placed over the die which has a cavity in the shape of the item to be formed. A punch to fit the cavity, with sufficient clearance for the metal, forces the brass into the cavity. It is sometimes necessary to go through two or more stages of 'drawing' to reach the required shape depending on the amount of distortion the metal is subjected to. A wide, shallow dish could be formed in one stage but a deep narrow item would need to go through several stages. (See the thimble dies in the next section).

Brass in its raw state has never been a popular metal for jewellery in modern times. In the eighteenth century a brass alloy which closely resembled gold in colour was devised by

Christopher Pinchbeck and labelled with his name. It was used a lot for cheap jewellery until well into the nineteenth century when it was superseded by electroplating.

Cheap cast jewellery is nearly always made of a lead alloy which has a much lower melting point enabling it to be cast into rubber moulds which are very cheap to make and can be used many times over. Pressed or stamped jewellery is mostly done in aluminium which is cheaper and easier to manipulate and can be given durable metallic or colour coatings.

The only time when the use of brass is justified is when its superior strength is required and even then it is usually given a plating of non-oxidizing metal such as gold or rhodium.

There is only one small area that the use of brass in jewellery making has not been fully explored, or made redundant, and that is in the use of great variety of tubes and extrusions that are available. You only have to look at the ends of the racks of extrusions in a non-ferrous metal store to set your imagination working overtime. A thin slice across some of these makes quite attractive earrings and pendants. Even the more mundane square and round tubes are transformed if sliced at an angle.

Using a hacksaw for this purpose is all very well for experimenting with different shapes but something much faster and more accurate is needed if they are to be turned out fast and uniform. Some small circular wood saws have a lower speed available so that non-ferrous metals can be cut using a fine toothed tungsten carbide tipped blade. The trouble with this method is that the blades are of such a thickness that you waste about as much material as you use and the noise is more than a little frightening. A much better method is to mount an engineers slitting saw in the lathe and fix the brass piece to the top slide. Using the pulleys or gear box you can select the most efficient speed. With the top slide you can select precisely the thickness of the slice and the cross slide will advance the metal to the saw at a controlled rate without your fingers getting anywhere near the blade.

Engineer's slitting saws are made of high-speed steel and are hollow ground so that the teeth are the thickest part of the blade. They come in a great variety of diameters, tooth size and hole size. The diameter will depend on the centre height of your lathe but most small lathes will accommodate a 10cm diameter blade. Taking into account the fixing clamp this will leave about 3cm for the maximum depth of cut which is enough to cope with most sizes of earring and pendant. At this diameter 1mm thickness will provide enough strength and rigidity and a 1mm tooth size will be fine enough to cope with the thickness of metal. A tooth size that is too coarse will jam if used at too slow a speed or too fast feed.

The most critical part of the operation is mounting the saw blade: it must run perfectly true. If it is the slightest bit out it will cut on only a few teeth per revolution and soon wear out. Most three-jaw chucks even when new are not often sufficiently accurate for this purpose and the diameter of the chuck restricts the use of the saw blade somewhat.

The mandrel of an instrument lathe is shaped to take collets and though the largest collet will probably provide enough gripping power for a 10cm blade it is an easy job to make an arbor with a collet shaped stem to fit the hole in the mandrel. If the stem is shaped first then fitted in the mandrel and the mounting for the blade turned to an accurate fit it will always run perfectly true whenever it is put back in the mandrel.

There is usually a small slot cut in the central hole in the blade to take a key which will prevent it slipping when in use. With clamping washers of 3cm diameter this should not be a problem but if it should arise, rather than go to the trouble of cutting a keyway in the arbor and fitting a key, drill a small hole in the arbor opposite the slot in the blade and fit a small steel peg in it.

When cutting the thread to take the clamping bolt support the die holder with the tail stock to ensure that the threads are cut accurately and so the clamping nut applies an even pressure to the blade.

With a model maker's lathe, or a larger one, the mandrel will be bored to take a morse taper but usually there is a chamfer on the mouth of the mandrel so that collets of one shape or another can be used. If you want to take the trouble to turn a morse taper on the arbor so much the better but it will still need a bolt screwed into it from the rear of the mandrel to provide sufficient gripping power. The most accurately turned morse taper is still a series of fine grooves left by the turning tool and will not mate perfectly with the finely ground recess in the mandrel. There should be enough area on the chamfer coupled with the bolt to give a firm grip on the arbor so the making of it will be identical to that for the instrument lathe.

To slice off parallel sided sections from tube or extrusions the brass can be clamped in the tool post and the cross slide moved forwards and backwards. The micrometer markings on the cross slide handle can be used to regulate the thickness of the slice.

A much quicker method is to fix a piece of steel or brass angle in the tool post and clamp the tool by hand by pressing it into the angle. If a stop is fitted to the end of the angle the brass can be moved quickly up against it after each slice is removed. It need not be an adjustable stop; the movement of the top slide can be used to vary the thickness, just a cut into the angle and the piece bent inwards will do.

Obviously the angle of the cut can be varied by rotating the top slide or just moving the position of the piece of angle supporting the brass but the most interesting shapes are made by cutting a piece at two different angles as shown in fig. 42A.

To get this result you could use the top slide swivel movement but as freeing the swivel also releases the top slide

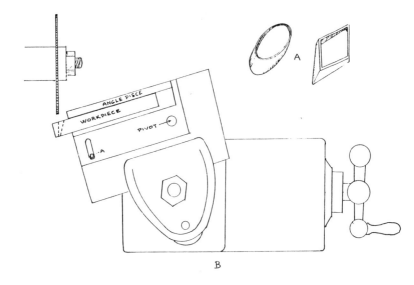

42   Device for slicing tube at various angles in the lathe

from the cross slide you would have to devise an alternative method of holding the top slide in place. It could be done by suitably shaped steel pieces gripped in the 'T' slots of the cross slide and the 'T' slots could also be used to hold stops to regulate the angle of the cuts. But it is all a bit messy and you would waste a fair bit of time trying to get the identical settings the next time you need to cut the same slices. What is needed is a moveable guide along the lines of that shown in fig. 42B. It consists basically of two slabs of metal, the bottom one having an extension that can be gripped in the tool post or a hole to take the tool post bolt so it can replace the tool post altogether. The top slab slides on to a pivot that is fixed in the bottom slab. Its degree of movement is controlled by the small peg 'A' in the semi circular slot. Holes at different positions in the base plate allow the pin to be put at different settings. The angle piece to support the brass can be soft soldered on to the upper plate if a sufficiently generous helping of solder is used. The left hand holds the brass in the angle and keeps the pin at one or other end of the slot while the right hand advances and retracts the cross slide. You can use the same sort of depth stop on the end of the angle as previously described. If you think that the blade is capable of making a quicker cut than the cross slide screw can provide remove the screw and slide the cross slide back and forth by hand.

One unusual use to which slices of brass tube were put was when there was a short-lived fad for square finger rings. These had slices of smaller tube soldered to one face in random patterns and were filled with different colours of epoxy resin then silver or gold plated. Cleaning the insides was a problem and supplying a range of sizes to fit different fingers was probably the reason for their brief life span but it may be worth resurrecting some time in the future.

A wide variety of shapes can be cut from thin brass sheet using the engraving machine and home made templates. The sheet can be supported on a wood or plastic backing and the pieces cut almost through then clicked out when the sheet is full.

Assorted slices in various shapes and sizes can be soldered together as shown in fig. 57, to make an unlimited range of designs. If they are set out on a charcoal block, all the joints fluxed, and the whole thing gently heated to solder heat they will keep to that temperature long enough for you to touch each joint with a very thin strip of soft solder. After washing in warm water to remove the flux they can be quickly dipped in Goddard's Silver Dip to remove any oxide caused by the heat and water then polished and lacquered or gilded.

To solder them in quantity several can be set out on a soldering tray and heated from beneath on a gas ring. Soldering trays made from a heat resisting material can be bought from a jewellery material suppliers or alternatively the trays used on ironing boards for the iron to rest on can be used or failing that a thickish sheet of mild steel though it is not so easy to control the heat with the latter.

If you should venture into the market for small novelties; round, square, rectangular and hexagonal tube can be bought in sizes where one is a slide fit into another. With the slicing device these can be cut to form the sides of a pill box and lid. A larger narrow one for the lid and a smaller sized wider slice for the box. These are soft soldered on to a piece of sheet and the surplus snipped off.

If the demand justifies it blanking dies can be made to stamp out accurately fitting tops and bottoms greatly reducing the amount of finishing work. The lids can be decorated in many ways: snippets of copper soft soldered in patterns or randomly, sections of smaller tube filled with coloured resin or paste stones, engraved if you have the machine, or initials cut out of thin sheet and soldered in place. Brass takes a good polish and, cleaned and lacquered, the boxes look very attractive.

Such items as the square rings really need plating to give them a reasonable life span but gilding or a thin coat of silver with lacquer on top is enough for earrings and pendants.

Gilding. Professional electroplating plant is very expensive but if you wanted to put a heavy plating on many items you would need the proper equipment to give you accurate control of the current and temperature etc. However for gilding and silvering, which is little more than a colour coating, far less sophisticated equipment will do the job. In fact, at its most fundamental, two large dry cells and an enamel saucepan are all you need, the most expensive item would be the cyanide salts. These are dissolved in warm water in the saucepan, the two cells are connected in series giving you three volts. A copper wire from the positive terminal is connected to an anode which can be a piece of fine gold or stainless steel and this is suspended in the solution. Fine gold makes the salts last longer because some of the gold is taken from the anode as well as the salts whereas with stainless steel the only gold available is in the salts. A wire connected to the negative terminal is bent into a hook on which is hung the article to be plated. It takes only five to ten seconds to build up a good deposit; the items are then washed in running water and dried on an absorbent tissue.

Most people get the shivers at the mere mention of cyanide but it is only dangerous if you swallow, inhale or get it in a cut. With good ventilation, plenty of running water, a pair of rubber gloves and reasonable caution none of these things will happen. You should always beware of getting over-confident and only undertake the work when you are not likely to get distracted.

If you need to do several items at once in order to speed the process you will need something a little more powerful than dry cells. A battery charger with a six and twelve volt range and a high and low setting on each range will allow you to vary the current to cover most jobs and is relatively cheap to buy. The salts can be obtained from various sources mentioned at the end of the book. The price will vary according to the price of precious metals at the time.

Silver. Fine silver is seldom used in the making of jewellery as it is too soft and in the thicknesses used in jewellery will change its shape with the lightest of pressure. Sterling silver is the most commonly used alloy of silver for jewellery in the U.K. It is 935 parts in a thousand pure and is the lowest quality that it is legal to offer for sale as silver in the U.K.

There are special alloys for spinning, drawing and casting but the standard sheet and wire obtained from the bullion dealers is alloyed with 75 parts copper which renders its workability somewhere between copper and brass.

From a jeweller's point of view the main advantage of using it is its classification as a precious metal. The mystique that this gives it allows a much higher price to be obtained than for a similar item in copper and brass, out of proportion to the cost of the material which in small items can be counted in pennies.

The disadvantages are that it oxidizes easily and that items above a certain weight have to be hallmarked which means that you have to make a quantity large enough to spread the cost of hallmarking so that it is less than the cost of the precious metal involved. It also means that you have to break off the manufacturing process, weigh, count, parcel up, post the articles and wait for their return before you can complete the order and in the meantime pray that you did not inadvertently use a bit of low grade solder somewhere along the way. I have often wondered how the motor industry would have survived if it had to send all its products away to a government department to be safety checked before they could be painted and sold and have the ones that failed the safety check rendered unsaleable.

The normal oxidizing process caused by exposure to the atmosphere is a negligible disadvantage with small items. On larger ones it can be prevented by lacquering, rhodium plating or airtight display packaging where necessary. Another form of oxidization which takes place when the metal is heated for annealing or soldering poses a more difficult problem. It is often called fire-stain and penetrates much deeper than ordinary oxide and is therefore more difficult to remove. It can be prevented by completely coating the item with flux but this is really only practical on one-off items because of the time taken in applying the coating and removing it afterwards. The alternatives are to remove it or cover it up. Fire-stain can be removed first by the use of emery paper and then polishing or, in less severe cases, just heavy polishing alone. Covering it up involves electroplating with either silver or rhodium. Silver plating has to be of sufficient thickness to allow for repolishing afterwards and the process takes time and adds to the cost. Rhodium does not require polishing but it is a much more expensive and critical process and robs the item of the 'silver look', giving it an appearance nearer to chromium than silver.

As most items have to be emeried and polished anyway more time spent on this process is usually the cheapest and most convenient solution. Often a judicious rub on a calico mop with tripoli will remove fire-stain, though being fiercely abrasive it will remove the sharp edges and leave a slightly worn appearance if you are not careful.

All your silver solder must be of hallmarking quality whether the items are to be hallmarked or not. For reasons mentioned earlier it is fatal to have a piece of substandard solder anywhere near the silver work bench. Solder labelled 'silver solder' as sold in an ironmonger's or D.I.Y. shop is likely to contain much less than the required amount of silver and should not be used.

Many of the items described in the copper and brass sections could just as easily be made in silver though the cost of the material and amount of waste must be taken into consideration. Also the finish is more critical: an unpolished edge on a copper ring costing pence would not be acceptable on a silver one costing pounds.

In silver jewellery physical strength is a greater consideration than with copper or brass. A weakness in the latter materials could be compensated for by using a heavier gauge of metal whereas with silver alternatives have to be found if the cost is to be kept within reason. Often this involves introducing curves and dome shapes instead of simple flat shapes.

An example of how this can be achieved simply is the case of the copper ring head in fig. 36A. To turn it into a silver bracelet link using a thinner gauge of material it could be made much stronger by slightly doming the punch. Though this would make the cutting edge less sharp it would not require a much heavier blow to stamp out the blanks so long as the doming is kept to a minimum. The dome can be ground on after the punch has been hardened and by trial and error gradually increased until the silver link will stand a reasonable amount of bending stress.

This basic link can be used for a variety of designs but first a method of linking them together must be devised. Soldering a loop on each end and hooking them together with a third ring would be one way but this involves soldering with the subsequent pickling and removal of fire-stain which should be avoided if at all possible. Another disadvantage to this method is that the bracelet tends to twist and flop about instead of lying flat against the wrist. You can solve the first problem by punching holes in the link instead of soldering on a loop and, by punching a hole in each corner and using two connecting rings instead of one, which prevents the bracelet from twisting

43   A punch and die for forming a slot at the end of each bracelet
link

when on the wrist but the end result has a very messy,
amateurish appearance.

A much neater solution involves the making of a punch and
die capable of forming a narrow slot at each end of the link, see

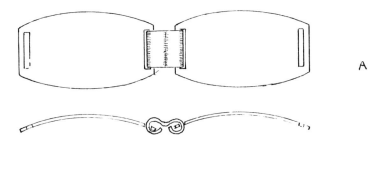

A

B

43a   Showing how bracelet links are fastened together and at 'B' the
joining link being formed

fig. 43. The links can then be joined together by a small strip of silver bent into a double loop as shown in fig. 43a. This will make a very strong unsoldered joining and result in hardly any waste metal.

Both punch and die can be made from 12mm diameter silver steel bar. If the link is the same size as the one described (25mm x 12.5mm and .5mm thick) then a slot 6mm long and 1mm wide would be about right. Of the presses described the home made quick-acting press would be best for this job as very little pressure and perfect accuracy is needed.

Dies as small as this one can be used in the fly press but you would need to make an adapter for the punch to avoid having a very thick shank on a very fine punch which makes the hardening and tempering more difficult. With the shank only slightly larger than the head it is much easier to bring the whole thing up to a uniform temperature. With a heavy shank it is difficult to avoid overheating the tip of the punch.

The adapter is a piece of bright mild steel bar about 5cm long, half of it being turned down to fit the hole in the press slide and the other drilled to take the new size of punch and a hole drilled and tapped to take the clamping screw. For clamping screws, where ever practical, you should use machine screws with a hexagonal hole in the head to take allen keys; these are ready hardened so the ends do not become splayed out by being pressed hard against the punch shank and the heads do not become chewed up with use. The diameter of the adapter should be such that a wide shoulder, about half the diameter of the shank, bears against the face of the slide to take the force of the blow rather than the shank bearing against the end of the hole. In the latter case the hole may become distorted and any punch that is not a close fit in the hole can be thrown out of alignment. A flat should be filed on the shank of the adapter for the press clamping screw to bear against, this prevents rotary movement of the punch and the surface of the shank becoming burred which, if it is a good fit in the hole, makes it difficult to remove. If the flat is also tapered so that it is deeper towards the head this will prevent it being drawn out of the hole should the punch become jammed. This also applies to the shank of any punch.

The quick-acting punch should be fitted with a depth stop with a fine thread so that you can control the amount the punch penetrates the die to a fine degree. This is necessary because the punch is a very tight fit in the hole it has made in the metal. It should be set so that the punch only enters the die sufficiently to sever the metal which can then be easily removed from the tip of the punch. The more it enters the metal the more difficult it is to remove and the greater the possibility of the punch being damaged in the struggle to remove it. In some cases a stripper in the form of a block of rubber can be fitted over the head of the punch to force the metal off but this prevents you seeing exactly where you are placing the punch which in most cases is necessary. The depth stop on the one illustrated in fig. 39 is the bolt screwed into the top of the press just in front of the slide. It restricts the downward movement of the handle and is locked in place by a nut.

After the shank of the slotting punch has been turned down to fit the press the business end is then turned down to 6mm diameter for a distance of about 5mm. It is then gripped in the vice and the end emeried to a smooth finish then coated with engineer's blue. Two parallel lines are scribed centrally 1mm apart to mark the width of the punch. The surplus metal either side is cut away with the hacksaw and finished with a fine needle file so that the tongue is an even thickness all over. Treat only the first 3mm in this way so that the remainder is left slightly oversize to give it strength. For the same reason leave a small radius at the base of the tongue where it joins the shank. The oversize portion can be ground down later if needed. The shorter it is to begin with the stronger it will be and the better able to deal with the task of forming the hole in the die without breaking.

Though it is not difficult to make such a small tongue even in thickness and in line with the shank the possibility of inaccuracy can be removed if it is left .5mm overthick and this amount removed in the lathe with an end mill. Though they are quite expensive to buy you can often find new ones in obscure sizes selling very cheaply in government surplus stores. For a facing job like this the size does not matter so long as it is in proportion to the job, in this case one of roughly 15mm would do. It is no good buying used ones, they have to be perfectly sharp, particularly to cut silver steel.

Though end mills made for use in a milling machine, they

can be used to a limited extent in a lathe. In the present case it would be mounted in the three jaw chuck and the silver steel bar clamped in the tool post. Leave enough of the bar so that it can be gripped firmly and can be lined up by eye with the end of the topslide. A 'V' block, if you have one will help in this respect. It is just a steel or cast iron square section bar with an accurate 'V' shaped slot cut along its length. Round material laid in the groove can be gripped more firmly. A piece of steel 'U' channel can be used as a make-shift. See fig. 20.

Set the lathe to run at its lowest speed but before switching on move the bar or the channel up to but not touching the end of the milling cutter, then move the cross slide forward past the face of the cutter to see that the bar is parallel to it. If it is apply some cutting oil to the cutter, switch on and move the bar into the cutter until it just begins to cut, then move the bar forward with the cross slide until the cutter has traversed one side of the tongue. When that side is clear of all saw marks turn the bar round and mill the other side until the tongue is the right thickness. You could square the ends off as well but being so fine the cutter might dig in and bend the tongue unless extremely fine cuts are taken.

If you made the die for such a small item out of a piece of plate or rectangular section bar a lot of material is wasted in just spanning the hole in the base of the press. If you use a small piece and screw it to a piece of mild steel you have then got the job of drilling, tapping and recessing four holes. A much simpler way is to make the die from a small piece of round bar. 15mm of 10mm diameter bar would do in this case. After the piece is cut off it is gripped in the three jaw chuck and faced off to a fine finish then turned around and drilled with a 7mm drill to within 2mm of the other end. If you have a boring tool fine enough the ends of the hole should be squared off so it is parallel with the outer face.

A holder has to be made for it so it can be clamped in the press. A piece of 2cm square bar long enough to be clamped on the press base is drilled in the centre of one side with a 10mm drill to a depth of 10mm then drilled right through with a 7mm drill. This will leave a ledge to support the die with a hole for the pieces to fall through. Drill and tap a hole half way down one side to take a clamping screw. If you do not have a machine screw of this small size make an ordinary slotted one out of silver steel and harden it because if you make any number of dies to fit in this holder the screw is likely to get a lot of use. Make it with as large a head as is convenient so it can be quickly tightened up with the fingers before the final twist with a screwdriver.

Finish off the head of the die with fine emery paper, file a tapered flat on one side and fit it in the holder in the press. Clamp the hardened and tempered punch in position and lower it to the die. Centre the die then clamp the holder to the bed. Bring the punch down and press gently, sufficient to leave a visible indentation on the die. Then remove the die from the holder and drill a small hole just large enough to take a piercing saw blade. The slot is then sawn out just clear of the indented mark then put back in the holder with the slot accurately lined up with the punch. Put a smear of thick oil on both components then lower the punch to the die, press it gently into the hole then withdraw it. If it comes away easily press it in again a little further then withdraw it. Continue doing this until the punch begins to stick in the hole. When that happens remove the die from the holder and clear out the burrs formed in the hole with a needle file and put it back in the holder. Do not be tempted to rush, a little at a time is the rule if you want to avoid breaking the punch and having to start all over again. When you are nearly through set the depth stop so that when it breaks through you will not slam the base of the tongue up against the die face and damage it.

Once you are through take the die out of the holder and run a burr held in the pendant drill along the back of the slot until the slot is only deep enough to hold two or three stampings before they begin to fall free. After hardening and tempering you are almost ready to begin punching the slots but first you need some sort of guide to enable you to put the slots in the same place every time. Very often when you are putting holes in a stamped out blank you can use a piece of metal from which the blank was stamped to act as the guide. Such is the case in this instance: a small piece of silver to fit round one end of the blank is cut from the waste material and soft soldered or superglued on the head of the die so that when the blank is held against it the slot is punched centrally and 1mm from the end of the link thus forming a 1mm bar at both ends of each link.

The strips for the joining links can be cut in the slicing machine described earlier. This is then cut into lengths long enough to form the links. The forming is done in three stages as shown in fig. 43a using a combination of round and flat nosed pliers. The two small rectangles and the circles in 'B' represent the ends of the flat and round nosed pliers respectively, showing how they are used to form the strip. The ends are curled in leaving just sufficient gap to allow the bars on the links to be threaded in then the link is finally closed using the flat pliers.

This is a quick and simple operation and hardly justifies a die but an order of only a dozen bracelets would require nearly a hundred of these to be made. The tedium and strain on the hands could be relieved by making the set of dies shown in fig. 45. As no cutting is involved mild steel would be strong enough and the shaping done with files. The pieces 'A' and 'B' can be made from one small block of mild steel by drilling two holes side by side then sawing the block in half then rounding the centre point with a file. The top piece will have to be drilled and tapped and a shank screwed in. The bottom piece could be soft soldered on to a piece of brass sheet to enable it to be held in position in a press. The punch to bend the strip into a 'W' shape can be formed on the end of a piece of round bar and the shank turned down to fit the press.

The old cast iron press originally used for embossing an address or emblem on note paper shown in fig 45a would be ideal for this as no great accuracy is needed and the punch does not have to travel far. Many millions of these must have been made because they still keep turning up at auctions and car boot sales and are sold very cheaply. If you can get hold of a few they can have one frequently used die permanently in situ and they do not take up much cupboard space. The one illustrated has a die for shaping a cup setting to take a 3.5mm stone which was always in use. The handles are spring loaded so it only takes a quick tap with the palm of the hand to operate it.

A bolt ring fastener on this type of bracelet though easy to fit would be out of character. The box snap shown in fig 44A would be much more in keeping and be almost invisible when the bracelet is being worn.

The shape of the piece of silver used to form the box is

determined by trial and error using a piece of copper sheet of the same thickness. Cut a piece roughly the right shape then grip it with a pair of flat pliers whose jaws are as wide as the inside of the box then bend the sides up and compress them with the parallel jaw pliers to sharpen the angle of the bend. Slide the box along the jaws of the pliers to a point where the back of the jaws can be used as a guide to scribe a line marking where the excess metal is to be cut away, see fig. 44B. The shallow end should be deep enough to allow free movement of

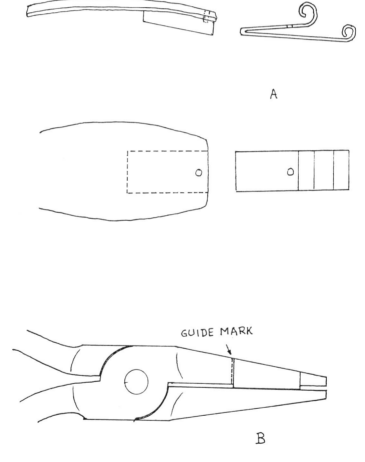

A

GUIDE MARK

B

44 'A' shows how the tong of the bracelet fastener is made and 'B'
     how the box for it is shaped in the jaws of the pliers

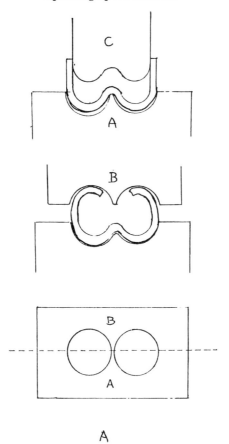

A

45   How the bracelet link can be formed with a punch and die plate

the end of the tongue: just over twice the thickness of the strip used to form the tongue. Once this point has been determined score the jaws of the pliers, this mark can then be used as a guide. If each box is bent up at this point any excess metal can be removed with the file so that both sides of the box end up flush with the back of the jaw and all the boxes will be uniform and sit flat on the link when they come to be soldered. The copper pattern can now be reflattened and used as a template to mark out the silver ones.

Before the box is soldered on to the end link the 'pip' that clicks into a hole in the tongue and holds the bracelet closed has to be fitted. There are two ways of doing this and the method used will depend on the quantity of bracelets to be produced. The first and obvious method is to drill a small hole about 1mm in diameter at the central point across the width of the link and about 1mm from the end. A piece of silver wire, a tight fit in the hole, is soldered into it then filed flush with the face of the link and trimmed on the underside until enough is left to make a positive grip in the hole in the tongue but not so much that it is a struggle to release it.

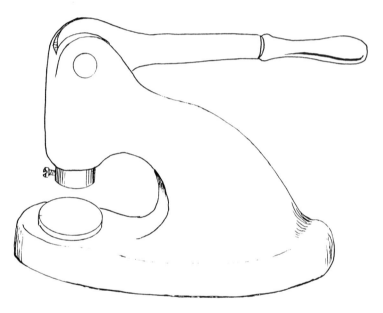

45a   An old embossing press that can be adapted for metal work

The job could be done a little faster if a hole punch was used to make the hole but most of the time would be taken up soldering the pin into the hole and trimming it to size and if the wire is not a tight fit in the hole it may move when the box is soldered into place.

A much quicker way to form the peg is to use a very loose fitting punch and die so that instead of punching a hole a peg is pushed up on the underside. The resulting recess on the face of the link can be filled with solder if it is thought necessary or it can be incorporated in the subsequent design on the front of the link. A guide will have to be fitted to the die plate so that the link can be quickly and accurately positioned beneath the punch and the travel stop set so that it prevents the punch penetrating too far and cutting off the peg. The home made quick-acting press is the obvious choice but a pair of punch pliers could be used if a stop was fitted. This could be done by drilling and tapping a hole through one jaw or through the handle just below the hinge and inserting a screw.

If the tongue of the snap is made from the same half-hard silver strip used for the connecting links a little time will be saved. But it must not be so hard that it is near to cracking when bent double or it will not last very long and if it is too soft there will not be enough spring in it. It can be made springy by hammering it but then you have to remove the hammer marks. Silver sheet can be bought in the half-hard state but if you are rolling your own a rough guide would be to bring it down to .75mm, anneal it then take it down to .5mm with one pass through the rollers. It is best to use the half-hard sheet from the bullion dealers because it is free of fire-stain whereas yours, unless you have a sophisticated annealing furnace, will not be.

If the hole in the tongue is to be punched this will obviously have to be done before the tongue is bent into shape which means some degree of trial and error in order to position it so it matches the position of the pip when it is bent into shape. It is a lot easier to shape up the tongue first then slide it into the box and allow the pip to scratch a line along the tongue; this will give you the exact position for the hole every time. The time you then have to spend drilling it instead of punching it will be more than offset by the time you would waste getting the punched hole to meet up with the peg.

The decoration that can be put on a bracelet of this type is almost limitless and allows full reign to your imagination and ingenuity. Engraving allows the greatest flexibility with the minimum of tooling but demands a certain amount of skill in wielding the gravers. Not the same degree of skill a professional engraver has because you can limit the scope of your design to fall within your capabilities and simple punches can be used for the shapes you find difficult to do with a graver.

Apart from using very sharp and polished gravers the secret

of engraving swiftly and accurately on a small item like this lies in having it firmly gripped but at the same time able to swivel so that the link can be moved into the graver rather than push the graver along the surface. It is very difficult to cut a line with a square graver and maintain the graver at the correct cutting angle: as the graver moves forward there is a tendency for the hand to lower slightly causing the graver tip to lift and eventually skid out of the cut and across the surface of the link leaving a scratch behind it. If the hand can be held steady at the correct angle and the metal moved instead there is much less likelihood of this happening. The quickest and cheapest way of doing this is to stick the link on the end of a short length of dowel using shellac, dopping wax or sealing wax. The other end of the dowel is domed and a recess cut in the bench to accommodate it. The wax is warmed until the link can be pressed into it. When the wax has hardened again the dowel is gripped in the left hand with the dome resting in the recess. With the little finger resting on the bench the link should be just clear of the forefinger and thumb. This way the little finger helps to keep the dowel vertical while it is being rotated and the thumbs can be pressed together to control the rate and length of the cut.

Sticking the link into the wax and removing it afterwards plus removing any wax that has adhered to the back of the link is fairly time consuming and it takes a bit of practice to keep the dowel vertical while rotating it. One way round this problem is to use an engraver's bullet. This device resembles a cannon-ball split in half and reassembled so that the top half is free to rotate while the bottom half rests in a circular leather cushion which prevents it rolling off the bench and also allows the whole thing to be tilted in any direction. Fitted to the top half is a vice with flat topped jaws in which a number of holes are drilled. Small pegs are fitted into the holes so that a great variety of shapes can be gripped in the vice. The jaws are operated by a removeable key so that there is nothing to interfere with the hands while the engraving is in progress.

The engraver's bullet is a very versatile instrument but relatively expensive. It is built to cope with the great variety of items a jobbing engraver has to deal with. For repetitive work on small, flat items a much simpler device could cope. There is a make of cheap hand vice available that can be easily converted to an engraver's vice, see fig. 46. If the wooden handle is removed and the metal stem that fits inside the handle fitted into a hole in a block of hardwood or metal it can then be rotated by the thumb and forefinger of the left hand. The top of the jaws are then filed flat and four holes drilled as shown, about 3mm deep to take·four metal pegs. With the metal pegs fully down in their holes a shallow groove is filed round the base of each peg so that it will firmly grip the bracelet link.

The only snag with this device is that you are limited to the items that are no longer than the width of the jaws. Also the travel of the jaws is only small so you are restricted in that direction too.

If a fair number and variety of items are to be engraved it would pay to make the following device which falls somewhere between the last device and the bullet. It is illustrated in fig. 47. It is made of brass because it is easy to work and will

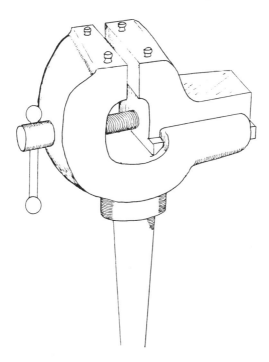

46   Hand vice adapted for use as an engraving vice

not rust as would a steel one with all the handling it gets. The main part is a 3cm length of 5cm diameter round bar. If you have to buy a piece the metal store will cut it off to the right length on a power hacksaw, or you might pick up an off-cut of the right length. A segment 3cm by just over 1cm thick is cut from the top. A slice is sawn from the segment so that when it is put back it leaves a 1cm gap across the centre. A hole is drilled through the centre of the loose piece and into the other side to take the screw that will close the jaws. The hole in the fixed jaw is tapped to take the screw and the screw should be a loose fit in the moveable jaw.

The 'T' slot in this case was made by first making a slot with an end milling cutter using the same set-up as was used to make the tongue on the punch of the slot punch then overlaying a piece with a narrower slot cut with a piercing saw. This is held in place with two screws though it could just as easily be soft soldered.

If it is difficult to grip such a large diameter in the tool post

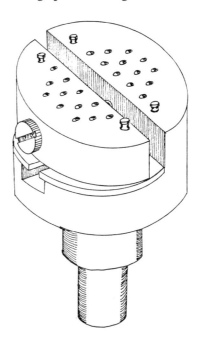

47　　Home made engraving vice

fit the supporting piece first and use that to hold it in the tool post. The support piece is a short length of 2cm diameter bar with 1cm of it turned down to a convenient size and tapped to fit a threaded hole in the centre of the body. The other end was turned down to fit the hole in a round cast iron block that just happened to be handy but any similar sort of base will do, even a block of wood with a piece of metal tube fitted into it to provide a smooth bearing. It is even better if you can fit a ball race there to give you frictionless movement.

The 'T' piece that fits in the 'T' slot is a short piece of round steel bar turned to a sliding fit in the slot with a short screw on the end to attach it to the underside of the jaw. The critical part is the length of the shoulder between the screwed portion and the underside of the wider piece. When the 'T' is screwed into the jaw then slid into the slot it should be a close sliding fit with no up and down play. In other words that shoulder should be as long as the thickness of the slotted sheet that forms the top of the slot. Any play here will cause the jaw to lift when tightened on a workpiece and may be forced down while you are engraving possibly spoiling the work.

When it is assembled screw the jaws up tight, fit it in the three jaw chuck in the lathe and turn the top to a fine finish. It just remains to drill the holes in the top and make a few pegs to fit. To decide where to put the holes it is best to wait until each job comes along and drill the holes to fit it.

Because you can not vary the thickness of the line, machine engraving either with the diamond point or a cutter is not really suitable for decorating articles such as this, for it gives a mass produced look to them. The only use would be to put a border line on them with the diamond point using a template made by the method described on page 62.

Even for short runs it is not practical to use the hand piercing saw for piercing designs; it is far too time consuming. The use of templates would speed up the scribing of the design and make them uniform; any attempt at speeding up the sawing would only result in a lot of broken blades and time lost replacing them. Neither is it worthwhile making a die for piercing an intricate pattern unless you can find other uses for it. A practical compromise is to use a simple die to make up a relatively complicated design by overstamping or using a combination of different simple dies and choosing shapes such that the piece stamped out also has a use.

When you get down to tiny stampings like these you are likely to lose a few and they find their way into the most unlikely places. One reason for this is the long drop from the die plate, through the hole in the base of the press and into the drawer beneath. Being so light they bounce when they land. With copper and brass you can always stamp out a few spares but with silver and gold you are throwing money away. One way to overcome this and save on die steel at the same time is to make the die plate support shown in fig. 48A. It is just a flat bed of mild steel with two thick strips screwed to it with a tapped central hole in each. It must be long enough to bridge the hole in the press – on a No2 it is 6cm diameter – and leave a piece for the clamps to grip. The die plates are screwed to a mild steel backing plate with holes in it to match the two in the two strips. The whole assembly is shown in fig. 48B. The bolt heads may have to be turned down so that they do not project above the surface of the die plate and scratch the underside of the sheet being stamped. One or both of the bolt holes should

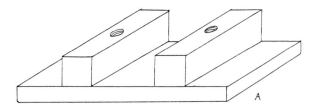

48   Method of mounting small dies

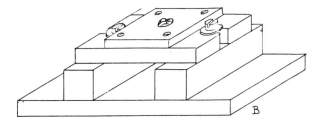

be extended to the edge of the plate so that you do not have to completely remove both bolts every time you change a die plate. Now a shallow box can be slid underneath to catch the stampings before they can go astray.

When one backing plate has been made with holes that match up to the base use it as a jig to drill two or three more; it is far quicker than marking out and centre punching every time you need one. The same applies to the die plate: drill the four securing holes in the first one and use that as a jig for drilling several more and also for positioning the holes in the backing plates. You can settle on one size of silver steel bar for stampings of up to one cm at their widest point. That used in the illustration was 3cm wide and 5mm thick and cut up into 4cm lengths. Plates of this size and thickness will have sufficient strength but not take much time to heat when hardening. At the same time you could also drill or turn a recess centrally in the underside through half the thickness of the metal so making it much easier to pierce and drill. If you make it 12mm across it will cater for any size up to your maximum of 1cm.

The little heart shape illustrated is quite simple to make. It could be used to pierce the link in the manner shown and the pieces stamped out used in several ways. With a peg soldered to the back they become small stud earrings; fixed to the end of a short length of wire or chain as drop earrings. Four can be stamped out of a circle to form a shamrock.

When making this die it is easier to make the plate first. To get the heart shape perfect you need to make a template first unless you happen to have an odd earring you can use instead of the plastic template that gem cutters use with heart shaped holes in graduated sizes which would save you a bit of work. The slightest difference in the two halves of the heart is quite noticeable particularly in such a small size. To avoid this you have to make half a heart first and use this as a template to make the template which is why it is much easier if you can find a ready-made one. Put a spot of superglue on one side and fix the finished template in position on the die plate. The engineer's blue will prevent it being too firmly fixed but firm enough to keep it in place while you scribe a deep line round it then prise it off. Drill two holes side by side at the top of the heart as large as possible without touching the line. Remove the rest of the metal with a piercing saw, keeping just inside the line then bring it to size with whatever needle files are appropriate. Then enlarge the heart from the back starting one mm from the face. In other words: when the stampings have moved down the hole for one mm they need to fall free. You need one mm to allow for sharpening the die by grinding the face when it becomes blunt with use. When this is done and with the fixing holes in place and recessed so the screw heads will not foul the material you can harden and temper it and screw it to the backing plate, bolt the backing plate to the support and put it loosely in place on the bed of the press.

A punch of this small size will have to be held in the adapter so select a piece of silver steel to fit the adapter and saw off enough so that you have about 2cm protruding from the adapter when the punch is fitted in to it. With a small punch like this for cutting thin material very little force is needed so there is no need to have a shoulder on the punch so long as the end of the hole in the adapter is flat and the tail end of the punch has the sharp corner removed i.e. a flat end with rounded edges, not dome shaped.

After turning down 1cm of the punch to a diameter that will just take the heart on the end, file a tapered flat for the clamping screw to bear on then fit it in the adapter in the press. Lower the punch and centre the die plate then bring the punch into contact with the plate and make sure that none of the heart shaped hole is visible around the edge of the punch then clamp the plate to the bed. Give the punch a gentle thump against the plate and with the use of a mirror have a look at the face of the punch. If you can not clearly see the outline of the heart continue thumping until you can. When it is clearly visible remove it from the adapter, file away as much of the surplus metal as you can without encroaching on the heart, then put it back in the adapter. At this point do not try to remove the surplus metal from more than the face. Make sure that the punch is accurately lined up with the hole then force it into the hole. Do not thump it in or it will jam, just a steady pressure is all that is needed. It should enter about half a mm before the burr builds up and brings it to a halt. From then on it is just a matter of removing the burr and a bit more of the surplus metal and repeating the process until about 3mm of the punch head is heart shaped. This amount will

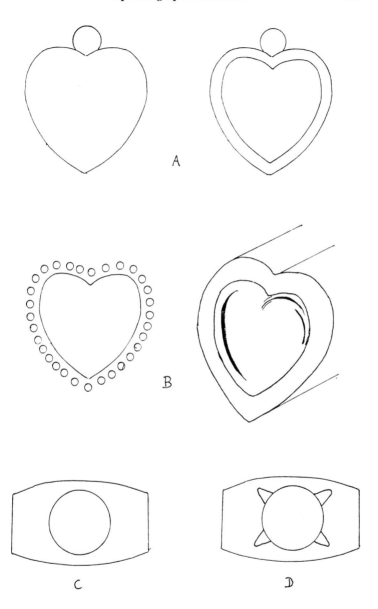

49 'A' and 'B' show three different uses of small heart shaped blank. 'C' and 'D' two ways of decorating bracelet blank

leave enough for future sharpening and leave you a clear view when you are positioning the punch for stamping the hearts. After hardening and tempering it is ready for action.

You can make further use of the punch and die just made by making the one in fig. 49A. This is a larger sized replica with a suspension loop attached. Again you make the die plate first and follow the procedure just outlined. Though it looks more difficult the only addition necessary is to drill another hole in the die plate to form the loop and the plate will form the shape on the punch. You have to take a bit of extra care not to damage the two sharp corners in the plate by the loop but that is all.

This stamping can be used as it is after a hole has been punched in the loop or the previous punch and die used to stamp out the centre. Alternatively a dome faced punch that loosely fits the heart in the first die plate can be used to form a raised heart on the second stamping or on the bracelet links. In addition if a border of indentations is placed around the heart on the first die plate either with an automatic centre punch while it is still soft or with a diamond burr after it has been hardened and a shoulder put on the doming punch a raised border will be formed around the heart if it is thumped hard enough, see fig. 49B.

The circle shown in the centre of the link in fig. 49C could be a dome formed in this way. It could also be a cabachon stone, but to set the stone in the conventional manner would require the making of a bezel which would have to be soldered on to the link resulting in deep oxide being formed. Assuming that the stones were identical in size – which is not always the case with low priced cabachons – the bezels could be cut from seamless tube the same way as the brass tube was sliced but it still leaves the work of soldering, setting and removal of oxide.

One way round the problem is to form four or six claws by raising them up from the body of the link either from beneath the stone or round it, as in 49D. If you raise the claws from beneath the stone you are restricted to opaque cabachons because the holes in the link will be visible through the stone. But if you raise them from outside you can use garnets and amethysts and such like stones. About the same amount of work is involved either way so your choice will depend on how you want the finished link to appear.

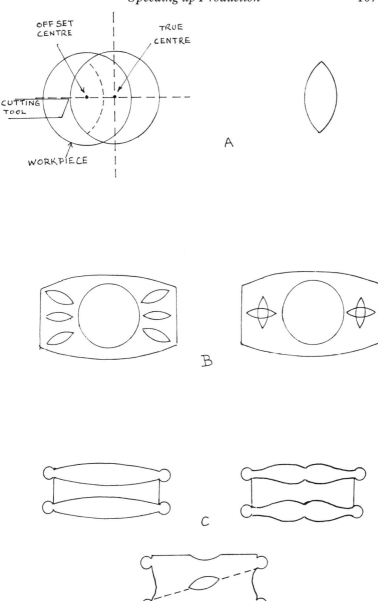

50 'A' Off-centre turning in the lathe. 'B' Two ways of piercing the bracelet link using the same die. 'C' Three alternate uses of the same blank

The dies use the same principle that was used to raise the shoulder on the copper rings: a cut is made on two sides and the flap forced up. The punch is a very simple affair if it is used to raise only one claw at a time and you can then vary the size of the stone by suitably positioning the claws but you are then left with the problem of doing that accurately. Making a pierced template and using it to mark the position of the claws on each link is the simplest way. The other drawback is that the die plate has to be cut away so that the claws already formed are not flattened when you push out the next one.

A punch and die plate to form them all at the same time is no more difficult than the one for forming shoulders, it just takes longer to make. The die plate is made first being the more simple of the two. Begin by coating it with engineer's blue then scribing a circle exactly the same size as the stone you are going to use then mark out the claws so that their roots fall outside the circle by the thickness of the metal to be used for the link allowing an extra fraction for any variation in stone size. If you are raising the claws from outside the circle the roots should fall just short of the circle for the same reason. In the latter case the holes left by the claws will have to be incorporated into a design, preferably pierced, so the reason for their existence is disguised. You can also do this by overstamping the hole with a punch of a different shape.

The shear on the punch need only be enough to cut the claws and raise the tip far enough for a knife blade to be inserted to bring them upright; that way is much easier to remove the link from the die plate and guide. This is most important if you decide to make a claw that tapers outward from the root, such as a fan or fleur-de-lis shape, because if it is pressed in below the surface of the die plate it will become wedged in and will need pressure from underneath to release it.

A punch and die to stamp out the simple leaf shape fig. 50A is one that is very easy to make and that can be used in several ways. In this case the punch would be the easiest to make first as it is just a matter of turning the end 5mm to a diameter the same length of the leaf then filing away the surplus with a flat file. This last part could also be done in the lathe using the four-jaw chuck and mounting the punch off centre as shown. With so little metal to be removed in the present case your only gain would be that the profile would automatically be uniform over the whole working part of the punch, whereas with the file you would have to take care but so long as the first mm or so is accurate to allow for future sharpening the remainder is not so critical. But off-centre turning would be well justified if you were making a much larger one such as the ring head, fig. 36B.

On the bracelet link the leaf shape could be used in two ways as shown in fig. 50B. In the first the two outer leaves are pierced and the centre one embossed using the same die plate but a domed, loose fitting punch. You could also pierce all three or dome all three or have different arrangements on alternate links. In the second it has been overstamped to form a four pointed star. The stampings can be used for applied patterns or, if the size is appropriate, shoulders on rings though separate shoulders are more appropriate to gold work than silver.

A small square punch and die can be used to form a lattice pattern and is very simple to make if a small piece of square silver steel bar is fitted into a mild steel shank then used to square off a round hole drilled in the die plate. An eight pointed star can be formed if the square is rotated through 45 degrees and overstamped.

The shape of the bracelet link so far discussed is pretty basic. The work and time required to make the die for a more elaborate link can be justified if the stampings are so shaped that they can have more than one use. The three links illustrated in fig. 50C will give an idea of what can be done. The cut along the dotted line on the first two links is made by placing the stamped link over the edge of the die plate by the right amount then stamped again. The third link can be cut with shears. In each case the resulting pieces can be turned into drop earrings or with the first two a light bracelet or neck chain can be made.

The link that has just been used to make a bracelet could be used with two short lengths of this chain to make an identity bracelet.

Chain Bracelets. If you have made the small circular saw for cutting up jump rings (see fig. 41) it can more than earn its keep if you make chain bracelets. Though all of the more

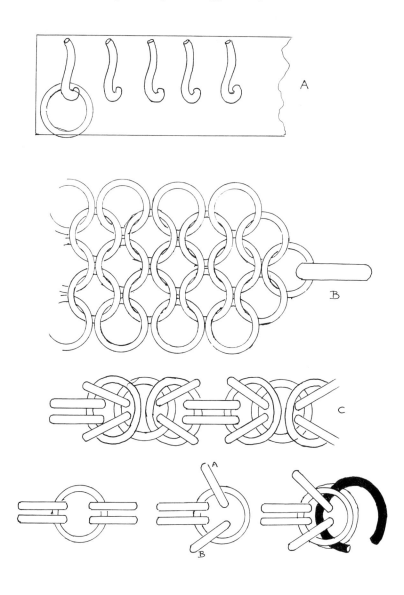

51   Making two types of chain bracelet

popular and simple types of chain are now made on automatic machines there are some types that because of their intricacy or limited demand have not been automated.

The chain mail bracelet is one of these and though it looks complicated, making it is almost like knitting with two pairs of flat nosed pliers and wire instead of needles and wool. It is time consuming but, because of its simplicity, it can be given to outworkers or you can press-gang members of the family into doing it while watching TV.

First you have to decide what width you would like the bracelet to be then, mostly by trial and error, work out the diameter of ring and thickness of wire necessary. The rings are not soldered so they have to be made from wire that has been drawn down to a hardness that will make them strong enough to resist an accidental tug but flexible enough to be opened and closed once without cracking. The wire should also be drawn through a drawplate that is in good enough condition to leave a polished finish on the wire because it is not possible to give the bracelet more than a light finishing polish when completed. If the wire is bought already drawn to size, and in the half-hard state, the bullion dealer's drawing plates will have given it a bright polished finish.

Apart from the pliers the only tool needed is the strip of brass or copper with a row of hooks on it shown in fig. 51A. This keeps the first row of rings in place while you add the second and keeps the bracelet extended while you add the subsequent rows. The only way to arrive at the spacing for the hooks is to make a short length of bracelet first then work from that. If the hook wire is a tight fit in the holes they can be soldered in quite easily and bent up afterwards shaping them as shown so they can be closed slightly to keep the rings from falling off. If you have a suitable punch to form the holes use that, then draw down the wire to fit. As a guide to size: if you use a wire thickness of .75mm and wind it on to a rod of 3mm diameter and make a bracelet of seven rows it should be somewhere between 20 and 25mm wide depending on the springiness of the wire.

The first row of rings are closed and placed on the hooks and the hooks closed. On the next row the rings are opened, threaded through two adjacent rings, then closed. This process is repeated for the rest of the bracelet. The neatest way

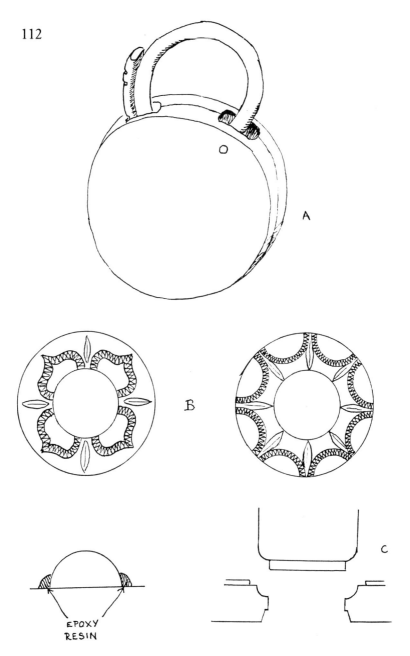

52 'A' A simple padlock using two identical blanks. 'B' Engraved patterns for the padlock. 'C' Making a simple setting for a cabachon stone

to finish off the ends is shown in the picture. The final ring on each end should be extra thick as it will be the weakest part of the bracelet.

If you use a mixture of rolled gold and silver rings you can introduce any number of patterns into the bracelet from simple banding upwards but you will need a coppery shade of rolled gold to get enough contrast.

The other design is much quicker to make. The diameter of the rings and thickness of wire should be such that when laid on a flat surface it keeps its shape. If the wire is too thin for the size of ring it looks like a pile of disordered rings and tends to get tangled.

To make a bracelet 6mm thick use a wire thickness of 1mm and the rod for the rings 3.5mm diameter. It is made by first closing six rings. Four of these are then looped together using two more as shown. This short chain is held between finger and thumb and the two end ones 'A' and 'B' folded back and the next two spread apart exposing 'A' and 'B' two more threaded through the exposed links and closed. The rest is just repeating this process until the chain is long enough.

You can again alternate with rolled gold and silver to give a variation. Another variation that works very well for a necklet or collar length chain is to graduate it by using progressively smaller rings of thinner wire.

A large bolt ring fastener looks quite well on either bracelet but their appearance is greatly improved by using a padlock. The conventional heart-shaped padlock will do and one way of making these is explained later, but they will be more uniquely attractive if the padlock in fig. 52 is used.

This has a double advantage: it is much more simple to make than the heart-shaped ones and it can be decorated with gems or engraving or a combination of both.

A suitable size for the body of the padlock would be 15mm so a circular blanking die and punch to make a blank of 17mm diameter is needed; this will allow for a one mm flange to be bent over in a forming die. Two of these pieces soldered together will give a thickness to the body of the padlock of 2mm.

A circular blanking die and punch are the easiest of all to make: all you need for the punch is a piece of silver steel bar the same diameter as the blank and turn a shank on it to fit the press. The die plate can be held in the four-jaw chuck and drilled and turned to a tight fit on the punch. I say 'a tight fit' because a tiny fraction is lost in scale when the metal is hardened and quenched and cleaned and a loose fit can end up a little too loose when finished which will leave rough edges on the blank that have to be filed off. Die plates that are formed using the punch or vice versa are automatically a very tight fit and the loss of metal during the hardening process is usually just enough to allow the punch to move freely in the die.

When the hole in the plate is the right size reverse the plate in the four jaw chuck and cut away the back of the hole to within 1mm to 1.5mm of the surface of the plate then harden and temper the two.

A circular blank of this size can have many uses and with this thought in mind it is as well to use a hefty section of bar for the die plate so that it will withstand a more powerful blow if blanks in a much thicker or tougher metal are required in the future. In the present case an 80mm length of 50mm by 6mm material would not be out of place.

The forming die can be made of brass or mild steel. The 15mm diameter hole in the die plate should have the sharp edge removed to ease the passage of the blank and likewise the face of the punch. If a hole is stamped in a piece of thin material with the 17mm blanking punch then this piece of material can be soldered or superglued to the face of the forming die so the blanks can be accurately and quickly centred over the hole.

If this seems like a lot of work for what may or may not be a good seller you only have to fit a hinge and catch to the two padlock halves and you have a small round locket, or push-fitted on to the ends of a short section of silver tube and one end soldered, and you have a miniature pill box.

When the edges of the two halves of a padlock have been trued up on a fine flat file, cut a slot in the flange large enough to take the tube hinge of the hasp then holding the two halves together in the tweezers solder them.

The hasp is made from a piece of round wire 3.5 to 4cm long and about 1.5mm thick. Slightly flatten a little over 1cm at one end and flatten a half cm of the other end to half a mm thickness. The latter is rolled up into a tube with round nosed pliers and soldered to form the hinge and the other end doubled up to form the catch. You will have to reharden it at the tube end by hammering it lightly on a block or there will not be enough tension in it to keep it closed. After it is shaped into a curve the tube is fitted into the slot, a hole drilled through the body and a hinge pin riveted in place. The hasp is closed and a hole to take the other end is drilled slightly back from where it touches the body then a slot is cut in the face of the doubled piece to form the catch and another near the top for the fingernail to press into to open the padlock.

For decoration a coloured cabachon surrounded by simple engraving looks best. Two designs are shown in fig. 52B. Unless you have used unusually thick metal to form the body of the padlock it will not be thick enough to be used as claws by pushing them out as for the bracelet link and as the metal has already been heated for soldering and fire-stain probably formed there is nothing to be lost by soldering on a bezel to take the stone. You can use a sliced off section of tube as described earlier or a bezel can be formed in two other ways. You can make a shallow cup to take the stone and solder it on; it will be easier to solder in place than the section of tube because you only need one spot of solder in the centre and if you accidentally solder it off centre it is easier to move than the tube which has a tendency to cave in under the pressure of the tweezers. Also, because the solder seldom comes right to the edge of the cup you won't be left with a shadow line of solder if you do have to move it.

The cup is a smaller version of the padlock half and formed in exactly the same way so nothing more need be said of it. The final version is a dome with the centre punched out which gives a decorative border to the stone and allows it to be firmly glued in place. If epoxy resin is used it fills the cavity as shown and locks the stone into place.

You do not have to go through the laborious process of doming small discs and then stamping the centre out if you make the small punch and die shown in fig. 52C. It can be used in a quick acting press as very little power is needed. The die is made from a short length of round silver steel bar whose diameter matches that of the blanks to be used, then the blanks can be centred very easily with finger and thumb. The bar is drilled in the lathe to the diameter of the stone to be used then a semi-circular recess cut in the mouth of the hole. The punch is made from a piece of the same bar and turned to match the die. The length of the cutting portion of the punch should be just enough to stamp out the centre and leave .5mm for sharpening so that it will not be difficult to remove the bezel from the punch.

When the punch is lowered on the blank it forces it into the cavity in the die, punches the hole, then shapes it into a dome. This latter action will stretch the hole a tiny fraction making it easier to remove from the punch.

Lockets. The market for lockets is not too fiercely competitive partly because of the time and skill required to assemble them satisfactorily. Judging by the poor selection on display in most jewellery shops a small manufacturer with a bit of imagination could make a comfortable living exploring this one area alone.

The round shape is by far the easiest to make because all the punches and dies can be turned up on the lathe as shown earlier in the case of the small, round padlock. The blanking punch and die for a larger more popular size of 25mm could be made and hardened and tempered in about two hours. The blanks would have to be about 28.5mm in diameter to give a thickness for the locket of 3mm with a fraction over for cleaning up the edges. The thickness of the metal used for a locket this size would need to be at least .5mm in silver to give it sufficient strength which would require a difference in diameter between the forming punch and die of 1mm.

The usual way of closing a locket by pressing it between thumb and finger will dent the locket in time if the metal is not thick enough or not domed slightly and a slight doming of the back and front greatly improves the appearance. This punch and die, as previously described, can be made from mild steel. They could also be made from brass, which would avoid the problem of rust forming, but if you anticipate using them to make 9ct gold lockets mild steel is recommended because of its extra hardness.

The doming of the punch can be done accurately enough in the lathe by first roughing it out in shallow steps then finishing it off with a file and emery paper. The difference between the centre of the dome and the sides need only be 1mm to increase its strength considerably. The inside of the hole in the die plate should be polished to ease the metal through and a spot

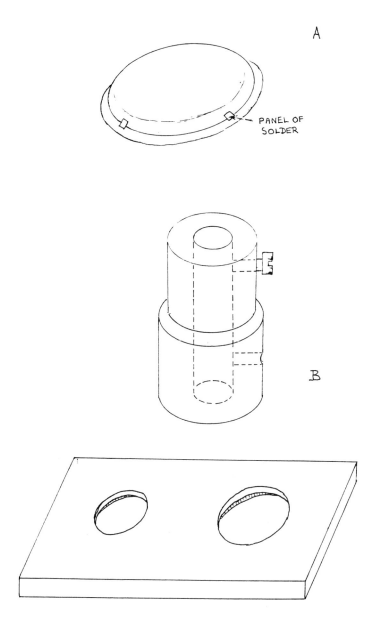

A

PANEL OF
SOLDER

B

53 'A' Soldering a locket side to the bezel. 'B' Double ended punch
and die plate

of oil will also assist, and the polish will be transferred to the rim of the locket reducing the finishing a little. If the gap between the punch and die is too large wrinkles will form around the edge so it has to be exact or slightly under to avoid this happening.

While the die plate is still in the four jaw chuck and before the inside of the hole has been polished a slight recess can be turned concentric with the hole to serve as a guide for the blanks. Use a blank to establish the diameter of the recess and make it an accurate fit. By doing this rather than sticking on a thin sheet with a punched hole in it, the concentricity is guaranteed and with a larger diameter like this you can end up with one side of the rim much deeper than the other if it is slightly out which means more finishing work or at worst a wasted blank.

When forming the rim the blank should be forced right through the die plate because it will spring open by a slight amount when through and this will enable it to be stripped from the punch when the punch is withdrawn.

After the edges of the front and back have been levelled on a fine grade flat file they are ready to be soldered on to the bezel, 'A' in fig. 53. These are made by stamping out a blank identical to the ones used for the front and back then stamping a circular concentric disc from the centre of this 4mm smaller in diameter.

To economise on die steel and to ensure that the punches and plates for these two blanks are always together the punch can be made as a double ended reversible one and the two holes cut in the same die plate as shown in fig. 53B. Remember to tap the clamping screw holes before hardening and tempering the punch.

When the backs and fronts are placed on the bezels ready for soldering it will be found that there is an excess on the bezel of about 2mm. This is intentional as it provides a platform for the solder and enables the heat to be applied evenly to the two parts so the solder will run into the join. Without it the dome would get hotter first and the solder run on to that part only. Use a medium to hard grade of solder so that it will not remelt when the hinge and other parts are soldered in place.

After the two halves have been soldered and pickled the

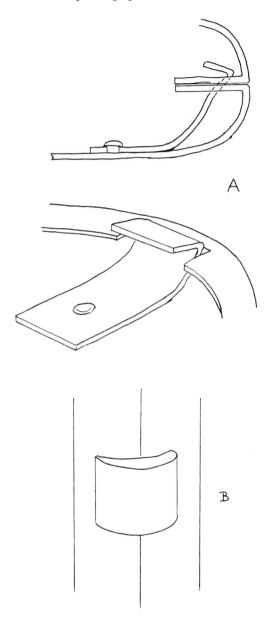

54   Two different ways of fastening a locket

excess bezel is snipped away with shears and finished off with the file. If you need to make a large quantity a blanking die can be made to remove this surplus metal and that in turn used to make the blanks for a smaller sized locket.

Before fitting the hinge some consideration should be given to the type of fastener for the locket. In the more expensive lockets an inner rim is fitted into one half and burnished slightly so that it is a tight push fit into the front bezel. Then two smaller bezels are made that are a push fit into the back and front to retain the transparent photograph covers. This involves a lot of extra work that could only be justified if a large quantity were to be made.

A simpler and quicker way of holding the two halves together is to make a small catch from silver strip that has been rolled enough to make it springy without being too brittle to bend. The strip is bent as shown in the diagram, fig. 54A, and secured to the back with a short peg which is soldered on to the back and passes through the hole in the catch and is then bent or riveted.

A small recess is cut into the rear bezel to keep the catch in position and a corresponding one filed into the front bezel so that the catch is not forced too far back when the locket is closed. A small gap is made with a half round file on the other edge of the bezel so the thumb nail can be forced between the two halves to open the locket.

There are two other ways of fastening a locket, both much simpler but also less reliable. One is to solder a small flap of metal to the front as shown in fig. 54B and bending it so that it grips the back when the locket is closed. As it is soldered into place there can be no tension in it and it is too small to harden effectively by hammering or squeezing with the pliers so eventually it will wear and cease to function. The other less unsightly way is to solder a short strip to the inside of the rear bezel and bend it outwards slightly so that it grips the front bezel when closed. This has the same disadvantages as the previous method. They could be overcome to a certain extent by using nickel for the strip which does not soften so much when soldered but then you would not be able to have the locket hallmarked and without the hallmark it can not legally be described as sterling silver.

An effective lining for the locket can be cut from adhesive

German, with buckle, late 19th century.
Gewerbehalle

19th century
German.
The Workshop,
Vol. 5

19th century
French.
The Workshop,
Vol. 5

Gold brooch. *The Workshop,*
1870

19th century English gold
brooch. *Spiers*

55   Old designs for brooches, pins and lockets

plastic sheet with a velvet or leather finish. The punch and die used for stamping out the bezels can be used for this purpose and also for cutting the transparent plastic photograph covers.

Before the catch is fitted the hinge has to be soldered in place. The two halves of the locket are placed together in alignment and a gapping file used to form a slot to take the hinge tubes. It should be deep enough to cover half the tube at its deepest point. A centimeter of seamless tube of a suitable outside diameter – about 1.25mm in the present case – is then soldered to one half of the locket. The centre third of the tube is removed with a file or piercing saw and a piece of tube that accurately fits this gap is soldered to the other half of the locket. If the two halves line up when placed together a broach is inserted into the tubes and rotated until the hole is tapered throughout. A matching taper pin is then inserted and pressed tightly home. If the locket is now opened and closed the pin should remain stationary in the outer tubes due to their larger gripping area. If this is not the case then the tapers do not match and the pin will have to be worked on until they do otherwise when the ends have been filed to match the contours of the locket the pin may rotate and expose the needle sharp points. Sometimes to avoid this happening the pin is snipped off short and the two ends of the tube filled with a silver plug.

After fitting the suspension loop and catch the locket is ready for decorating and finishing. For some reason hand engraving alone is the most common form of decoration and yet the blank face of a locket will take just about any form of decoration: embossing, gemsetting, enamelling or an enamelled plaque fitted. Locket makers of the past were not so shy in this area and just about everything was tried with some very beautiful results. Perhaps some of the skills have been lost or were much cheaper then: pave setting the front with turquoise or seed pearls would not today be worthwhile on a silver locket, but there is still plenty of scope for those with more modest skills.

The elaborately embossed lockets of the past (see fig. 55) had the design carved into the head of the doming or forming punch; this was then hardened and a deep impression made in a brass or bronze die block so that the front of the locket was shaped and embossed at the same time. A very old brass die block for shaping and embossing a small heart shape is shown

56   An old brass forming die

in fig. 56, with a lead impression taken from it alongside.

It takes a great deal of skill to carve such a design but a larger one as with the present locket using a simpler design made up of geometric shapes could be applied to the punch using smaller hand punches but it would need a heavier press than a number 2 or several blows with annealing in between with the accompanying risk of a miss strike.

An easier way of doing it is to build up the design with smaller elements such as the heart embossed on the bracelet link. The only restriction here is that the pattern in the die block has to stand proud of the surrounding metal so that the current embossing does not foul any previous embossing. This is not a problem if the embossings are fairly well spaced, and then intervening spaces can be filled with simple engraving or wriggling with a flat or lined graver. If the embossing is done before the bezel is soldered on, the piece can be put back on the doming punch and passed through the die again to correct any distortion the embossing may have caused.

Applying designs by soldering separate pieces on can be a messy business and fraught with the difficulty of removing any excess solder afterwards. It is far easier to make a separate piece, a cross for instance, solder four pins on to the ends of the arms, punch four holes in the locket front and rivet them over from the inside. As the inside of the locket is usually covered with a lining the rivet heads will be hidden. You can then put a perfect polish on to the locket front and put the cross on afterwards. This method also solves a lot of problems with enamelled designs and little groups of stone settings can

A

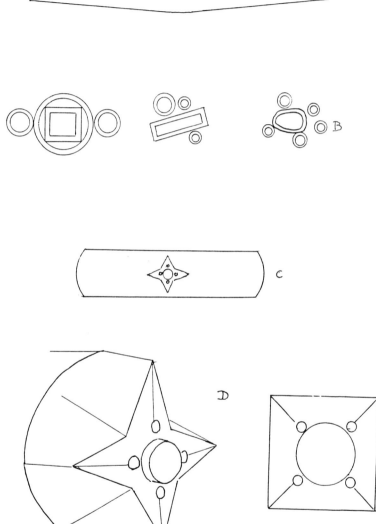

57　'A' Ring blank. 'B' Tube slices used as decoration. 'C' Punched star setting. 'D' Two punches used to form a star type setting

be fixed in the same way.

Oval and heart shaped lockets obviously require a lot more handwork and filing to make the dies but apart from that the procedure is the same as for the round one. A bit of forethought about the size of the shapes, particularly the oval, can result in the dies having several other uses. Commercial cabachons for instance go up in standardized shapes and sizes; if an oval blanking die for a locket is shaped to conform to these standards a blank can have a flange turned up with a forming die so that it can be used as a setting for such a stone which could become the basis for a brooch. The blank that is stamped from the front and back bezels also has its centre stamped out and is used to retain the photographs and transparent cover in place and the centre that is stamped from this can also have a flange formed on it and is about the right size for a cabachon dress ring.

Rings. A very useful shape for the shanks of rings is shown in fig. 57A. If it is made about 6.5cm long it can be shortened down to cover the more common sizes and stretched a little when bent up and soldered to cover most of the larger sizes as well. The die plate is made first by marking out then drilling a series of graduated holes which are then joined up with a heavy duty piercing saw to remove most of the centre; it is then filed to size. As it can be used for many different styles of rings and in 9ct gold as well it is liable to get a lot of use so it is as well to make the die plate from fairly thick material, 6mm at least. It will mean that the filing will take a lot longer but this can be reduced by drilling overlapping holes on the underside slightly bigger in diameter than the widest part of the shank through half the thickness of the metal.

The punch can be made from a piece of the same material then fixed to a mild steel shank by two or three screws. If a smear of superglue is put on it before assembling enough will enter the screw holes to prevent them working loose with the vibration. With the die plate hardened and the punch very nearly to size remove the final shaving of metal by mounting them in the press and forcing the punch into the die.

A shoulder piercing die similar to the one for copper rings can be made for this shank and the oval setting to take cabachons made to sit neatly in the tips of the shoulders and the curve of the shank providing three solder points so making it a strong ring as well as attractive.

Sections of silver tube can also be mounted on the shank to make some interesting designs, see fig. 57B. If the cavities are oxidised or filled with matt black paint it gives a very nice contrast and solves the problem of cleaning or polishing these awkward places.

The shanks can be rounded up using a piece of dowel held in the vice as with the copper rings but for thicker or tougher material a ring bending machine like the one in fig. 58 is needed.

Being a specialized machine with a very limited market it is comparatively expensive but once you have the dimensions it is quite simple to make the parts with the use of a lathe and a little help from a welder. The main body is a 10cm length of

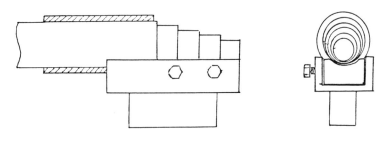

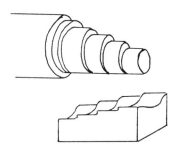

58   Ring bending machine

mild steel tube welded into an 8cm length of mild steel 'U' channel. A small block of mild steel is welded beneath to give it rigidity and to enable it to be held in the vice when in use. The hole in the tube should ideally be 28mm diameter though 1mm either way will not greatly affect its efficiency. The piece of bar to fit it is mounted off centre in the four jaw chuck and the four steps turned at the one setting. Leave enough spare at the other end for the handle to grip. The steps in the block are cut in the same way as the punch for trimming the ends of copper bracelets: held in the tool post and cut with a boring bar in the three-jaw chuck. The boring bar cutter is adjusted to the various diameters. As can be seen these are larger than the corresponding steps on the mandrel. After they are cut the edges are rounded off with a file so as not to mark the metal being bent. If the handle is made quite heavy usually its weight alone is sufficient to bend the metal which allows you to operate it quite quickly. The shank strip is fed in between the block and the mandrel and the handle moved up and down. The curve or size of the ring depends on which step is used. The two screws in the channel are to position and clamp the block. Packing pieces are placed one or the other side of the block to line it up with the mandrel then the screws tightened.

This machine is indispensible when it comes to bending very thick wire: it will bend with ease stuff that you can hardly touch with the ring pliers. If you choose the right step on the mandrel it will make the ring perfectly round and closed so that you only need to put the piercing saw blade through the join to square the faces and it is ready for soldering.

One such ring that you would need this machine for is made from thick 'D' section wire and has one or three small, star set, brilliant cut stones set in it as shown at fig. 57C. Cutting star settings requires a fair amount of skill but in this case there is an easy short-cut. A punch is made from a short length of silver steel and the head is filed as shown in fig. 57D. The circle in the centre is a short peg for fitting into the hole that is drilled into the ring to take the stone. The four small circles round the peg are very fine holes drilled to a depth of .5mm. With the ring held on the triblet the peg is inserted in the hole and the punch given a sharp blow with the hammer. The result will be a star setting with four pips ready formed with which to set the stone. With the star design being hammered on to the convex surface of the ring the top and bottom arms of the star will not register very well unless they are so shaped that they match the curve of the 'D' to a certain extent.

The other punch, fig. 57D, performs the same function but leaves a neatly indented square instead of a star. With a three stone ring you can use the star punch for the centre with a square either side for variety.

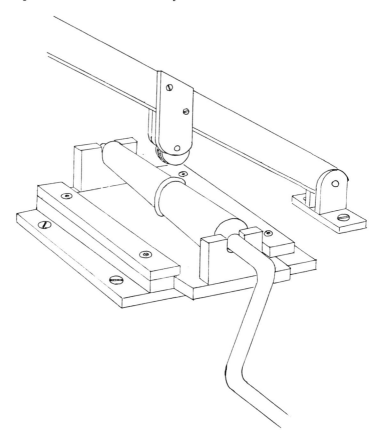

59   Fast acting ring stretching machine

Rings as heavy as this are difficult to stretch on an ordinary ring stretching machine. A machine that will cope easily with these and any others and cannot be beaten for speed of operation is shown in fig. 59. It does not appear in many catalogues but again it is one that can be made in the workshop with the help of a lathe. The base of the slide that carries the mandrel is usually dove tail shaped and slides in a matching groove machined in the base the same as the cross slide and top slide of a lathe. A 'T' slot built up with strips of mild steel bar as shown works just as well and is far easier to make.

In use the ring is slid on to the mandrel. A wheel with a groove to match the profile of the ring is fitted in place and the arm lowered. Pressure is applied with the left hand while the right rotates the handle of the mandrel and keeps the ring tight on the taper at the same time.

Thimbles. These were once a purely utilitarian article but have now entered the realm of collectibles, the search being for unusual or offbeat designs. This has created a market for the small manufacturer.

They can be spun into shape from a flat disc mounted in a high speed lathe. A metal former in the shape of a thimble is clamped in a chuck and the disc pressed tightly against it by a running centre held in the tail stock. A tool similar in shape to a wood chisel but with a rounded and polished end is held against a support in the tool post and the polished tip of the tool is pressed against the rotating disc and gradually forces it on to the former. Shallow shapes are not too difficult to make in this way but deep ones like the thimble require a lot of skill to coax the metal into shape. If the shape is too deep intermediate formers are used and the metal annealed after each one.

The problem with forming the disc into a thimble in the press is similar to that with spinning: the outside diameter of the disc has to be reduced in size to the opening in the thimble without wrinkles. A toolmaker would probably do it in two stages, first making the disc into a shallow dish then in another die make the final shape. The precision work needed to make the second die, which has to keep the shallow dish in perfect shape while a punch passing through the centre of it gives it its final shape, is beyond the scope of a small workshop and a relatively inexperienced machinist.

The third way of doing it requires very little skill but a fair amount of time. You make a series of progressively deeper dies and anneal the disc after each operation.

The blank for an average sized thimble should be about 4cm in diameter and .5mm thick. As the accuracy of the circle is not critical it can be scribed with dividers on the sheet and cut out with shears. Later, if the demand justifies it, a blanking die can be made for the purpose.

It will take between five and seven sets of dies to turn the blank disc into a thimble depending on the thickness of the metal, its elasticity and how soft you can make it. This is not such a daunting task because the first two or three sets can be made from hardwood or Tufnol – a form of thermosetting plastic with material embedded in it – as they are not subjected to much wear or strain. The remainder can be made from brass or mild steel.

The first set should raise the sides up by about 20 degrees from the horizontal. More than that and the wrinkles that begin to form will be too deep to be flattened by the die. A shallow recess is turned in the face of the female half of the die to enable the blank to be quickly and accurately centred over the recess beneath.

As only the downward pressure of the press is needed in this operation – the blanks do not become stuck in the dies so no power is needed to raise the punch – it is not necessary to bolt either piece to the press so no flanges or shanks are needed. This greatly simplifies the making of them particularly if hardwood or Tufnol is used for the early stages. The only problem that this creates is the centering of the punch over the blank. This can be overcome if a lip is turned on the top face of the die as shown in fig. 60A.

It should be 42mm in diameter and the body of the punch made 42mm as well. It will be found that the plastic fittings used for joining 1.5 inch plastic waste pipe will fit snugly over the punch and lip so guiding the punch into the centre of the blank. To ensure an even pressure on the blank the top end of the punch should be faced in the lathe so that it is perfectly flat and at right angles to the sides. The point of the punches should be left flat until the very last stage so that the applied pressure is spread over as large an area as possible. If it is domed the pressure will be concentrated in the centre of the dome and the metal will probably split. After each stage the disc will have to be thoroughly annealed.

When the blank has reached the halfway mark, about 50

degrees, a tougher material will be needed for the dies because more pressure is needed to eliminate the wrinkles that develop. Also the working surfaces of the dies and punches will require a light coating of grease or oil to prevent the blank becoming jammed.

As the angle of the sides increases the thimble becomes

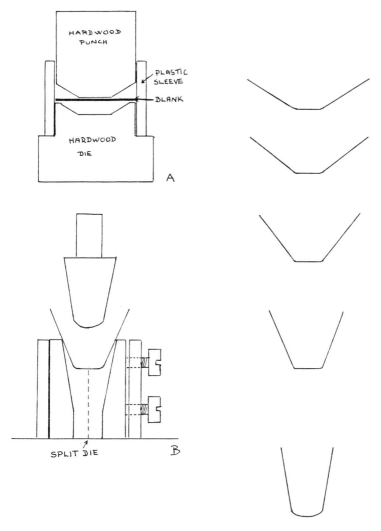

60   The stages in forming a thimble shape

more firmly gripped in the die because it acts like the morse taper in the lathe. In the final stage this has to be overcome by splitting the die as shown in fig. 60B and held together with the collar and clamp screw. If this is not done it will be impossible to remove the thimble from the die. It will also be firmly fixed to the punch but advantage is taken of this by mounting the punch complete with thimble in the lathe and turning off the ragged base of the thimble. While it is still in the lathe the whole surface is smoothed with fine emery paper and all traces of fire-stain removed. It will be found that the heat generated by the emerying will have caused the thimble to expand slightly and will be easy to remove from the punch.

If any grooves are required in the pattern to be applied to the sides of the thimble they can be cut with a lathe tool before the finishing process has loosened the thimble from the punch.

Small knurling wheels are available, or can be made, that are larger versions of the graining tools used for creating a neat row of beads on a bezel setting. These larger versions are used by silversmiths for raising a row of beads round the edge of a cup or similar shaped article. Two grooves are turned side by side and the knurling wheel, mounted in a holder and clamped in the tool post, is pressed firmly against the ridge between the two grooves. The lathe chuck is rotated by hand to give better control over the placing of the beads. The pressure on the knurling wheel is gradually increased until the beads are fully formed.

The indentations on the head of the thimble that catch the top of the needle and prevent it slipping can be drilled in the engraving machine using a plastic or brass template with concentric circles of holes drilled in it. The reduction arms are set to reduce the template to the size of the head of the thimble and the cutter stop adjusted so that the holes only penetrate half way through the metal. They can be more laboriously applied with an automatic centre punch with the sharp point blunted or in sets of three or four using a specially made punch.

Another type of thimble can be made without a top on it. The appropriate shape is cut from sheet and curved into shape with the ring pliers. After the seam has been soldered the shape is trued up by pressing it into a die similar to the final stage in the previous one. While it is still stuck on the punch it is mounted in the lathe and the top trued up and a small step cut to form a seat for a cabachon stone. The stone when set in can be left plain or a few indentations made with a diamond burr.

Spoons. These are another item that are not classed as jewellery but fall within the scope of a small press and are part of most jewellers' stock in trade. The neglected areas are where the demand is limited such as souvenir spoons for special places, or small towns that carry a coat of arms or special emblem, and christening spoons with an initial on the handle.

Spoons that are to be used as such need a fairly deep bowl so the blank has to be cut first and shaped afterwards but for the type of spoon just mentioned a shallower bowl would do and this can be cut and shaped at the same time using a punch like the one illustrated in fig. 61.

Because it is dome shaped the cutting edge is fairly blunt so it could not be used to form the hole in the die plate so the plate would have to be made first. Because of the bluntness the

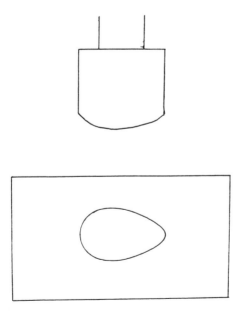

61 Punch and die for simultaneously forming and blanking a shallow spoon bowl

plate would have to be fairly thick to withstand the extra pressure needed to stamp out the bowl. The extra work that this entails can once again be reduced by turning a circle in the underside of the plate slightly larger than the length of the bowl and through half the thickness of the plate.

An attractive handle can be made for the spoon from 3mm square wire. One end is shaped to fit against the bowl, the other end is split into a 'Y' shape to take whatever is needed and a twist put in the centre by clamping it in two hand vices and giving them a half or full turn.

Gold. Nine carat gold comes in a variety of colours and alloys and most are malleable enough when annealed to be worked with the dies and tools described in this section.

The relatively high price of gold makes economy and minimum waste of primary importance resulting in much thinner sheet and wire being used than would be the case with silver. As it is a much harder material than sterling silver this is mostly quite practical.

Before the refinement of the centrifugal casting process, and the invention of the rubber mould which made mass production possible, most quantity production of jewellery was done with drop hammers and presses. In Europe in the nineteenth century the art of ornamental die making reached its zenith when gold and silver and even base metals were forced into unbelievable three dimensional shapes for all types of jewellery. Today, what remains of the skills, seems mostly confined to coin and medal manufacture. Even there a lot of the handwork has been taken over by the three-dimensional pantograph machines which are probably now computer controlled. The only skill and handwork is now concentrated in producing the pattern for the machine to trace and the hand-finishing of the dies.

The main limitation to casting is in the thickness of wall that can be cast and it is in this area that there are niches for the small manufacturer. Lockets are one such item but what has been said in the section on silver applies equally to gold.

Earrings. Simple delicate earrings can be easily and quickly made using a few basic elements. It is a good policy initially to confine your use of gemstone to a fairly limited range of sizes and shapes because it is then worth making dies to produce the settings for the stones which can be used to ornament a range of different items.

Before deciding on which sizes and shapes it is best to enquire into the prices of the different stones you are likely to be using because quite often a half or a millimeter smaller can reduce the price out of all proportion to the size due to the scarcity or abundance of certain sized crystals.

The punch and die in fig. 62A produces a four claw setting

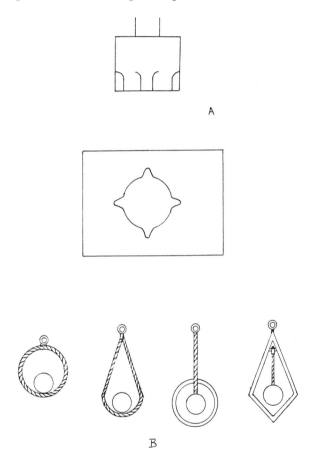

62 'A' Punch and die for blanking a simple four claw setting. 'B' Simple earring designs

for a 4mm cabachon but when formed into a cupshape becomes a setting for a 3.5mm brilliant cut stone. Both of these can be used to produce quite a range of simple earrings a few samples of which are shown at fig. 62B. All are made from fine round wire which has been flattened in the rollers then twisted. Before being twisted it has to be thoroughly and evenly annealed. If you use a propane torch for this purpose you will need to go over it twice to be sure no spot has been missed otherwise the twist will be uneven at this point and probably break before the remainder is complete. To make the twist, one end of the wire is clamped in the vice and the other in the chuck of a hand brace. The wire should be kept under slight tension while the handle is being turned. The twist may form unevenly at first but evens up the more it is twisted.

The die plate to produce the setting is obviously the easier of the two to make being just a drilled hole with the claws made with a piercing saw. This is then used to shape the punch as has been described before. To shape it into a cup you need only a blunt ended punch with a ninety degree taper on the end. The matching cavity in the die plate is made by drilling a 1mm hole then enlarging it with a conical burr. The guide in this case is a small piece of .5mm nickel sheet with a blank stamped out of it then superglued centrally over the cavity. As it requires very little power to shape the cup the small embossing press shown in fig. 45a and described on page 96, is adequate for the task.

Hook wires are the cheapest and simplest way of attaching earrings to ears. They can be bought quite cheaply but sometimes the price is kept down by using wire that is too thin to last very long or the finishing process has been neglected and the point that passes through the ear is left rough. By making your own you eliminate these risks and the possibility of running out half way through an order. They are easy enough to bend up with round nosed pliers but it is not easy to make them all identical this way. This is overcome by using the simple jig shown in fig. 63A. It is just a 10cm length of hardwood dowel with two holes drilled in one end, one of 6mm diameter and the other 1.5mm into which short lengths of round bar of the same diameters are forced. They need only project above the surface by 1mm. The wire to be used is snipped into 30mm lengths and a 1.5mm loop turned on one

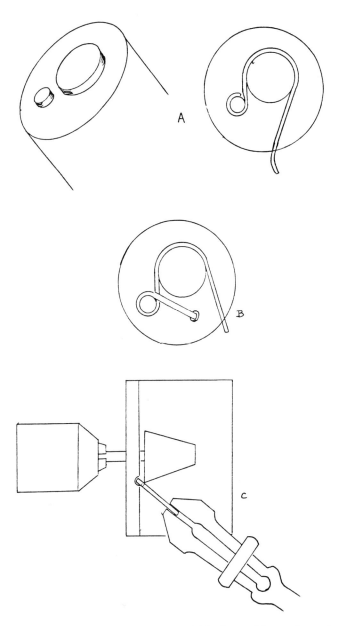

63 'A' Jig for making hook wires. 'B' Jig for making safety wires.
'C' Method of cutting a groove round the end of an earring stem

end with the round nosed pliers. The loop is placed over the small rod and the wire bent tightly round the larger one as shown in fig. 63A.

A similar arrangement of rods can be fitted into the other end of the dowel with the addition of a small piece of tube and on this you can produce wire with the safety hook, see fig. 63B.

Hook wires with a bead in the end can be shaped up on the first jig if the bead is soldered on first. The cost of this type can be reduced if a small domed cap is used instead of a bead. These can be made in the quick-acting press using a 2.5mm round punch and die with the head of the punch domed slightly. Being so small they can be stamped from any piece of scrap rolled down thin enough. They can also be soldered to the front of the safety wires to give them more finished appearance.

The small setting mentioned earlier was made to take a 3.5mm faceted stone when shaped. With a stem to take a scroll clip on the back it makes a conveniently sized stud for practical day wear or for people with their ears pierced in more than one place. Again the fittings can be bought cheaply but usually because they have economised on the metal with the consequence that the clips do not grip very well for long and you almost need a pair of tweezers to hold them.

The stems are easily made from wire snipped to length but making one end flat for soldering and the other rounded so that it passes easily through the ear and then forming a groove to prevent the clip slipping off could not be done efficiently with needle files.

Small grind stones are available to fit the pendant drill. One of these is shaped like a shortened cone and if driven by a small induction motor can be made to perform these operations very quickly. Apart from the motor the only other things needed are a wooden base board and a short piece of angle iron. It is arranged as shown in fig. 63C. A hole is drilled in the angle iron slightly larger than the stem of the grindstone. A small indentation is made with a centre punch or burr just behind the sharp edge of the grinding wheel. One end of the ear wire is touched against the grinding wheel to remove any burr and give it a flat end for soldering. It is then clamped in a pin vice and the other end rounded on the stone;

then that end is placed in the small indentation for support and the stem brought into contact with the corner of the grinding wheel and quickly rotated until a groove is formed all the way round the stem. The operation is speeded up quite a bit if a quick release pin vice is used like the one shown.

The strip cutter described on page 39 can be used to cut the sheet into lengths for the clips and then snipped off into 19mm lengths using the flat topped snips with a mark scribed on their side 19mm from the cutting edge of the jaws.

The hole to take the peg should have a small recess surrounding it to guide the peg into the hole; without this it is extremely difficult to fit the two together behind the ear. The hole has to be accurately centred side to side and end to end or the clip will be lopsided or weak. One way of doing all three in one movement is to make the small punch and die shown in fig. 64A. They can both be quickly turned up on the lathe and made to fit the quick acting press. The die is made 19mm in diameter, exactly the length of the strip for the clip. A recess slightly deeper than the thickness of the strip is turned in the face of the die to within 2mm of the edge then a hole the same diameter as the wire stem is drilled exactly central and a small recess cut round it. Using the centre hole as a guide two lines are scribed across the face of the die equidistant either side of the centre hole and as far apart as the width of the strip. Where these marks cross the 2mm rim at the edge of the die a gap is carefully filed away so that the strip will fit in them. If the strip is held between finger and thumb and placed in the gap it will be central in both directions.

The punch should be just long enough to pierce the strip and have a thickened base so that the metal around the hole is forced into the recess surrounding it. To form the wings of the clip an old pair of round nosed pliers can have one jaw ground down to the inside diameter of the wing then when the end of the strip is gripped in these and given one turn identical wings can be formed on all the strips. The wings should touch each other in the centre so that if a broach is pushed through the hole and given a couple of turns a groove is made between the wings which will keep the wing in line on the stem when it is being worn. They can be gripped in the round nosed pliers, one jaw in each wing, to make polishing quick and easy.

An alternative way of making the clip is to make the

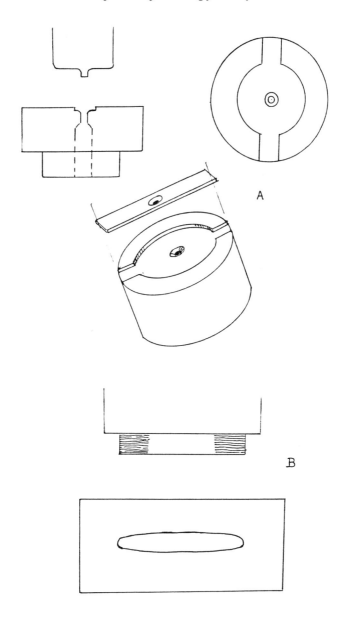

64 'A' Punch and die for punching a recessed hole in a butterfly fitting. 'B' Punch and die for making the blank for a butterfly fitting

blanking die shown in fig. 64B. Stamping the blanks is much quicker than preparing the strip and it gives a nicer, tapered shape to the clip when the wings are rolled up but it entails a certain amount of waste in sheet.

Hollow domed studs have hardly ever been out of fashion and make a good bread and butter line. Most of those available are made from a hollow, spherical bead soldered on to a stem and do not sit as well against the ear as a flat backed one. These take longer to make but can be priced according to their superior quality and a variety of sizes with differing heights of dome can be made with little extra work.

The backs and fronts of the studs are made from the same round blank. Doming the front reduces the diameter so that when it is placed on the back it leaves a surrounding shelf which nicely accommodates the solder. You can increase the height of the dome and make two differently shaped and size of stud using the same sized blank. By making another blank half as big again in diameter you would have a range of four with a minimum of die making and what there is can be done very quickly on the lathe. A blank of 5.5mm diameter would give a shallow domed stud of 5mm and a high domed one of 4mm which are popular sizes.

As it takes only two or three blows with the hammer to form such a small dome in the doming block with a doming punch there is not much point in making a die for this though the face of the blanking punch could be given a slight curve to start the process off. It means that the backs will be slightly domed as well but this has the advantage of making them better able to withstand the inward pressure when the clip is forced on to the peg.

After the fronts have been domed they are rubbed on a fine file to level the edge then the backs and fronts fluxed and placed together on a charcoal block face up and a panel of solder put on the shelf which should be even all round. As many as the block can accommodate can be quickly soldered one after the other if the flame is directed so that the following one is being heated while the current one is being soldered.

With these small sizes it is very noticeable if the stem is slightly off centre. One way to avoid this and at the same time make a stronger join is to drill a hole centrally to take the stem. This can be done accurately in a small lathe, an old watchmaker's lathe adapted for the purpose is ideal. A collet is needed that is a good fit on the dome of the stud. If one the right size is not available an old worn one can be softened and a hole turned in it to take the dome. It need not be rehardened, there will still be sufficient spring in it for the purpose. Watchmaker's lathes are not normally equipped with a tail stock chuck for drilling purposes as they are not accurate enough but a make-shift one can be made by turning down the body of a pin vice until it is a sliding fit in the tail stock hole. With a drill in the pin vice and the pin vice clamped in the tail stock the tail stock body clamp is loosened so that it can be quickly slid backwards and forwards to drill the holes.

After the stems have been soldered into the holes and the studs have been pickled and cleaned the surplus metal on the back is snipped off and the edge cleaned up with a needle file held against the rough edge while it is gripped by the stem in the lathe then finished off with fine emery paper ready for polishing.

With hollow items like this if there are any pinholes in the soldering air will be drawn into them as they cool; any subsequent heating will cause the air to expand and if it can not get out the hole fast enough may cause the item to explode. If you are in any doubt drill a small hole somewhere before reheating.

Larger studs can have the stems butt soldered on to the back because any slight inaccuracy in centering is not so noticeable.

The hallmark, of necessity in this case, is placed on the stem and is so small that it is unreadable to the naked eye and it often flattens or roughens the stem so then it has to be trued up with an emery stick making it even less readable so it is adviseable to stamp 9ct on the back disc with a small cutting punch before assembly. A block punch should not be used because it will distort the metal too much making it difficult to match the two halves together.

Another simple stud that can be made from a round blank to take a small cabachon is shown in fig. 65A and B. If the blank diameter is the same as the distance between the tips of opposite claws on the blank for the four claw setting described on page 135 then that blanking punch can be used to shape this setting. All that is needed is a mild steel die plate with a

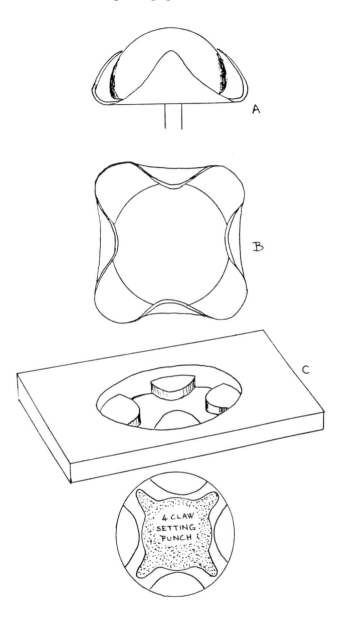

65 'A' and 'B' Simple setting for a cabachon stone formed from a circular blank. 'C' Die plate for forming the setting

hole shaped as shown in fig. 65C with a round recess to centre the blank. When the blank is pushed through the die it comes out as shown and only needs a stem and the stone setting in by bending the tips over the stone with a blunt knife blade. In this case it would take a 4mm stone.

As well as being used as a stud it could be used on the twisted wire earrings in place of the four claw setting. It also looks quite nice on a small split shank ring which can be sold with the studs as a set.

Punches and dies like the four claw setting ones may look perfectly accurate when finished but will seldom mate properly in any position other than the one in which they were made. In other words you could not rotate the punch through 90 degrees and expect it to match the die in that position. It might be quite close a match, enough to fool you but you would soon learn of your mistake when the punch jammed solid in the die or broke off a delicate corner so it is essential always to file or grind a mark on the shank of the punch and a corresponding one on the die plate so that you always match them up correctly.

Four claw cup settings to take stones larger than the 3.5mm one are made in the same way but on larger sizes the sides begin to look noticeably blank and have a utilitarian appearance. This can be offset by making the centre a square instead of a circle. When shaped into a cup a peak is formed between each claw which adds a little more sparkle and interest to it. See fig. 66A.

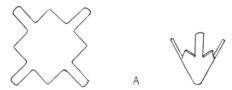

66 'A' The blank and the formed setting for a four claw setting for brilliant cut stones

The blanking punch and die for an oval four claw cup setting is no more difficult to make than the one just described but it is more difficult to judge the size so that when it is shaped into a cup it will match the size of stone you want to use. To guarantee accuracy you need to make the shaping die first then you can use an actual stone as a gauge to check when it is the right size. Rather than try to make a flat bottomed hole in a thick plate it is much easier to use a plate whose thickness is the same as the height of the walls of the setting, pierce the shape out with a saw then bolt it to another piece to form the bottom.

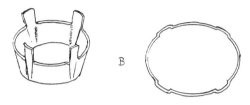

66a   Larger type four claw setting

When you have got it to the right size and shape to take the stone, allowing a little for the thickness of the gold, you file up a punch to match. It is worth taking the trouble to shape the two so that the claws are embossed on the side of the cup as shown in fig. 66a. It looks a lot better and allows the stone to seat properly.

The shape of the blank has to be arrived at by trial and error. Scribe one as accurately as you can judge from the dimensions of the hole in the die on a thin piece of brass. Cut this out with a piercing saw, clean up the edges with a needle file then use it as a template to scribe another one. With the forming punch and die lined up and clamped in the press, soften the blank you have made and place it very carefully over the hole in the plate so it is absolutely central. Bring down the punch until it just touches the blank to help you judge if it is central and if so press it into the die plate. If your judgement was spot on and the cup perfectly formed then you can cut out the other template and use that to scribe the outline on the blanking die plate. If not, you can now see what adjustments need to be made on the template to get it right the next time but when you have made the adjustments and cut out the new blank remember to use it as a template to scribe out another on the brass before you shape it into a cup or all your efforts so far will be lost.

As before the blanking die plate is the easiest to make because it can be cut out with a piercing saw; from then on you repeat the processes described earlier.

The setting can be used as it is for a stud setting but on an ear drop, pendant or ring it will need to have an oval stamped out of the base to get more light to the back of the stone. And as a ring setting it would need to be made from a slightly thicker gauge of gold.

Often it is possible to try out a new idea this way. Making the forming dies first in softer metal and using a template to cut out the blanks by hand then, if it looks like being a potential winner, make the blanking die and punch using the template as a guide.

Another use for this setting is to make an oval hollow stud by using a plain forming punch so that the claws are not embossed, then, by snipping off the claws and soldering the cup on to a backplate you have a nice three dimensional shape with a flat front to carry any decoration you care to put on.

The casting process is ideal for making rings, for the most intricate can be produced with relative ease. But very thin rings produced for cheapness are soft and fragile due to the structure of cast metal whereas pressed and rolled items of the same weight are comparatively strong. A simple setting that was used for a range of birthday stones is shown at fig. 67A. Here the shoulders and settings are formed in one piece so they only have to be trimmed up and the shank soldered on. The blanking punch and die were both cut from 3mm thick silver steel strip because they would be used to cut very thin sheet so little pressure would be put on them. The punch was then screwed on to a mild steel shank. Though, as can be seen from the forming punch and die, 67B, it was used to form a rectangular setting, it could just as easily form an oval by altering the shape of this punch and die. When it is forced into the forming die the corners of the central square are forced upwards to become the claws. The shoulders rise up at the same time but these are bent back into position with pliers. The narrow ends of the setting will have a ragged edge due to the contraction; this is removed with a needle file giving more prominence to the claws.

The soldering on of the shank is made easier if a groove is filed in the tips of the shoulder for the shank to rest in. The

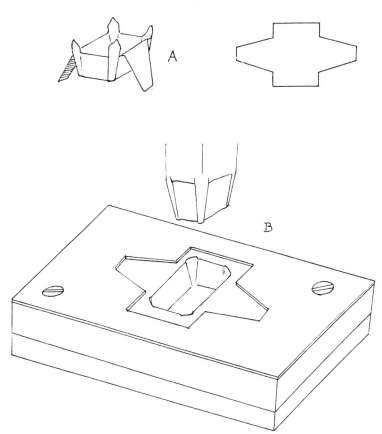

67 'A' Rectangular four claw setting and the blank. 'B' The forming punch and die plate with guide

setting is then pressed into a charcoal block upside down, the claws forming an anchorage. The shank will then rest in the filed grooves and be kept in position while being soldered.

Though the blanking and shaping of these small settings could be done in the fly press a much smaller, slower acting press could cope and give better control. The Pinfold ring sizing machine is capable of doing this work and as they have been replaced for the most part with later inventions, can be picked up quite cheaply. The only alterations necessary are the removal of the brass ring which is held in place by two bolts. The bolts are then used to tighten down the die clamps which are just two lengths of mild steel with a slot in them to take the bolts. See fig 5. The other alteration which was necessary before it could be used as a press was to fit a small block at the base of the ram. This has a small tongue which is a close sliding fit in the keyway which runs the length of the ram. Originally the tip of a small screw rode in the keyway but this was worn and not accurate enough to stop any rotary

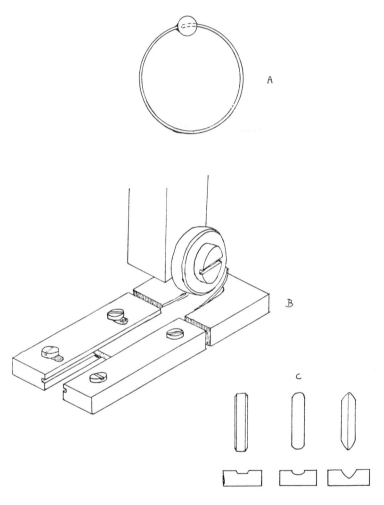

68   'A' Simple sleeper earring. 'B' Device for shaping wedding ring earrings. 'C' Rollers for obtaining different profiles

movement of the ram.

Sleeper earrings are always in demand partly because of their popularity and partly because the hinged variety break very easily. A sleeper that can be made very easily and quickly and without a hinge is shown in fig. 68A. It is merely a piece of springy gold wire with a gold bead with a hole in it soldered to one end. When bought the beads usually have a hole in them so it is only a matter of enlarging it to fit the wire.

The wire is drawn down to .75mm and left hard and springy then tightly wrapped around a piece of 8mm diameter round bar. When it is released it will spring open to between 12 to 15mm which is about right for an average sleeper. They are snipped off with the shears and the ends squared up with a file then closed but not too tightly. A 2.5mm bead is slid over one end and soldered on to the other with low melting point solder. In use the free end is pulled from the bead, twisted sideways and threaded through the lobe, then put back in the bead. So long as it is twisted sideways it will always keep its shape.

Larger ones can be made in the same way but using thicker wire. They can also be made from twisted wire but after twisting the wire should be drawn through a couple of holes in the draw plate to make them smooth.

Another popular earring is the wedding ring type so called because of its resemblance to that article. These have been produced in large quantities in silver on automatic machines at very competitive prices. But gold ones because of the higher cost of material and smaller demand are made in much smaller quantities so the price is much less competitive giving the small manufacturer an opening if he can make them.

A limited number of designs can be made on the quick acting press using the same principle as the ring bending machine. If a steel disc of the same profile and diameter of the earring is used to press a strip of thin gold into a matching channel cut in a strip of steel the gold will take on the shape of the channel; fig. 68B. If one end of the channel is curved to match the diameter of the disc then the strip will be curved around the disc at the same time as it is forced into the channel. By feeding the strip into the gap between the disc and the channel and repeatedly pressing the disc into the channel the strip will loosely wrap itself round the disc and be formed into the required shape. The springiness of the metal will cause it to open slightly enabling it to be easily removed from the disc. Several discs with their matching channels are shown in fig. 68C. The punch clamping screw in the quick acting press, fig. 39 has a shoulder turned on it that matches the hole in the discs and is just long enough to allow the discs to rotate when the screw is tightened.

The discs are drilled and turned on the lathe and given a polished finish with fine emery paper. The channel is cut with a boring bar in the three jaw chuck using a cutter to match the profile of the earring. The small slab of mild steel in which the channel is to be cut is either clamped in the tool post or on the cross slide using packing pieces to bring it up to the height where the channel will be cut to the correct depth. So that the curve in the end of the channel matched the disc the distance between the centre of the boring bar and the tip of the cutter should be the same as the radius of the disc plus the thickness of the gold.

The slab is fed into the cutter from the rear so that when the cutter comes into contact with the slab they are in effect travelling in opposite directions. If you do it the other way round the cutter will dig into the slab and something will break.

It is easier to grind the cutter to shape first, cut the channel then turn the wheel to fit the channel rather than the other way round because you would have to keep removing the cutter from the boring bar, grind it a little then reset it at the right diameter. It is only necessary to cut about 1cm of flat channel in front of the curve.

The large object in the illustration is the strip guide with, at the top, one of the channel pieces bolted in position with its matching wheel to the left. Without the strip guide it would be impossible to keep the strip in perfect line with the channel. It is made from two pieces of mild steel bar with a fine groove .1mm deep and .5mm wide running the length of one edge. This is cut with a slitting saw mounted on an arbour and fitted in the three jaw chuck. The guide piece is gripped in a machine vice bolted to the cross slide.

The guides are held in place by the four socket headed machine screws. The hole in the guides through which they pass should be overlarge so that the guides can be adjusted to match the width of the gold strip being used.

The strip cutter described in fig. 17 is ideal for cutting the strips of gold because they will all be precisely the same width which is necessary if they are not to jam in the guide. With everything assembled and in place use some copper strips first to make sure the channel is in the correct place to form the curve when the strip is fed in. If the wheel is too far from the curved part of the channel the earring will not follow the curve of the wheel. You will need something to push the strip along between the guides with a 'V' in the end so that it does not slip. With the pusher in the left hand and the press handle in the right it only takes a dozen quick movements with the handle and in seconds the earring is formed.

Various profiles can be made, fig. 68C shows a 'V', 'U' and a flat bottomed 'U'. The sides of the channel must always be at a slight angle otherwise the strip will jam in the channel.

The cross is an eternally popular motif and they are stamped out by the thousand on automatic presses so you may think it not worth while trying to compete. But being so popular you are bound to get asked for them so it is as well to have at least one in your armoury if only to stop your customer having to go elsewhere for this item and risk losing business. The punch for a small one is difficult to make because you cannot cut it with a piercing saw from thin bar and screw it to a mild steel shank: there is not enough width in the body to take a screw hole without making it dangerously weak. So it has to be carved on the end of a solid round bar of silver steel. For this reason you have to choose a size that can have multiple uses and a shape that is a little out of the ordinary. The punch and die shown in fig. 69 produce a cross that is 3cm long, not counting the loop, and 2cm wide. This size is not too large to hang on a sleeper or hook wire and not too small for a small pendant. It is about the right size for a charm or putting on a locket or tie pin so it is bound to show a profit one way or another and once you have made it you have got it for good.

The die plate is a simple piercing saw job but the proportions need to be spot on because any inaccuracy is strikingly obvious on this shape so it is best to make a template first so you can get it exactly right before you mark it out on the die plate.

When the punch has been turned to size smooth the face to a fine finish with emery paper, cover it with engineer's blue and

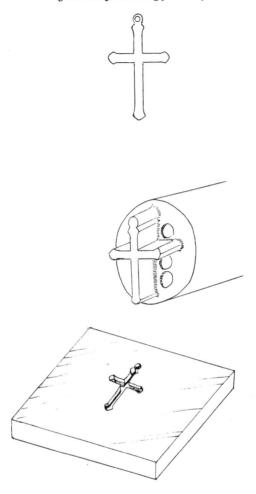

69   A cross blank and the punch and die used to stamp it out

use the template to mark out the cross. Next put a centre punch mark between each arm of the cross in such a place that the largest possible drill can be used without touching the cross. That will enable you to remove the maximum amount of metal with the least effort. Using files and burrs remove as much of the remaining surplus as you can. To get far enough into the corners of the cross you may have to use a flat graver broken off short and used like a cold chisel with a hammer.

When it is as near as you can make it clamp it in the press making sure that the clamping screw is engaged on the tapered flat you have filed on the shank. Oil the hole in the die plate and centre it beneath the punch. Use an eye glass to be certain it is spot on then drive the punch into the plate. At this point put the clamps on the plate and clamp it hard to the bed because it is likely to be firmly attached to the punch and you will need to use the upward movement of the press to release it. It was not clamped first off because the punch will have a self-centering effect on the die when it first comes into contact and if it is bolted down it cannot move. Once the punch is removed from the die it is just a matter of cleaning off the burrs and repeating the process until you have about 1.5mm of the punch shaped then hardening and tempering it.

Cuff Links These have been slow sellers since jeans and T-shirts were introduced as the national dress. As with pendants just about anything can be fixed to a cuff clip and sold as a cuff link. With this in mind you are one jump ahead if you can make your own cuff clips. The spring loaded variety are a complicated affair and considering the demand not worth the trouble. They are best bought in when needed but are quite expensive in gold due to their weight. Short lengths of chain with a miniature torpedo or dumbell on the end were the standard at one time but were the devil's own job to thread through the button holes with one hand and just about impossible to remove at the end of a social evening.

A simple compromise is shown in fig. 70A. The beauty of this device is that if you have made the blanking die for ear scrolls the same blank will serve as the tail piece if made in a thicker gauge of gold. The curved piece that is soldered to the back of the link can be cut from strip using the punch and die made for trimming the ends of copper bracelets. One end is rounded up and a hole punched in it and a strong loop soldered to the tail piece with the opening just clear of the soldered join so that it can be opened, threaded through the hole and closed.

A nice chunky head of minimum weight can be made from the bracelet link on page 88 if a forming die is made similar to the one for forming the cup on the oval four claw setting to give you the result shown at fig. 70B.

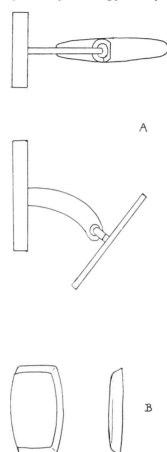

A

B

70   'A' Easily made cuff link fitting. 'B' Hollow head for a cuff link

Padlocks. These will be popular for as long as chain bracelets are worn and there are some small firms who make it their main line. The usual way of making them is to stamp out two identical blanks and solder them on to a rim as shown in fig. 70. Before soldering, the imitation screw heads and keyhole are stamped on the front then the hasp is fitted as described on page 114. The most difficult part is the soldering and next is bending the rims so that they match the blanks every time. Soldering the rim on to the back is not so difficult because the solder can be placed on the inside in the angle between the back and the rim and it will flow round that angle quite easily but soldering on the front while keeping it in line with the rim is not so easy because there is no angle or shelf to guide the solder and distribute the heat more evenly between the two pieces. All these uncertainties are eliminated if the back and front can be made with half the rim ready formed on each. Fig. 71B will show what I mean.

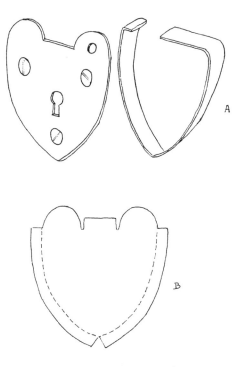

71 'A' Padlock front and rim. 'B' Blank that eliminates the soldering on of a rim

The forming die plate is made from a piece of 5mm thick mild steel and the outline of the finished padlock scribed on to it. You are better able to get the proportions right if you make half a template first and use that to scribe the outline of both halves. Most of the metal can be drilled out then finished off with saw and files.

The forming punch is made next using the same template and when it is a good fit in the die plate on the side that you scribed file away enough from the sides of the punch to allow the sides (rim) of the padlock to be folded up when the punch pushes the blank through the die. The punch should be of sufficient length to push the blank right through the die so that when the punch is withdrawn the bottom face of the die pulls the blank off the punch.

The face of the die has the edges where the folding takes place rounded off with a file. It is now ready for a trial. A blank template is made using the half template already made to scribe the shape on a piece of brass sheet then the pieces of rim are added on either side and between the two curved pieces. This is then sawn out and used as a template to draw two blanks on a piece of copper sheet the same thickness as the gold sheet used to make the padlock. Cut one of these out and line it up on the die plate in the press and push it through with the punch. If it comes out right cut out the other one and shape that as well then put the two halves together and see if they match. If they do you can use the brass template to mark out the blanking die plate and so on, if not you will have to make another template with the necessary adjustments. When it is working well it takes only minutes to stamp the blanks and push them through the forming die. This can be done on the fly press but the Pinfold is strong enough and easier to control when forming.

The next job is to make a small hand punch to stamp the imitation screw heads on the front. This is made from a short length of round silver steel about 1cm diameter with a 45 degree point turned on it. The point is filed away until it is the same diameter as the screw head then two semi-circular depressions cut in it with a reverse cone burr then hardened and tempered. The forming punch clamped in the vice is used for a support while the screw heads are punched on, using the minimum of force so as not to distort the padlock front.

The keyhole can be made from a round hole punch with the slot made with a piercing saw or a small punch and die can be made for it to fit into punch pliers. After the two halves are levelled off on a fine flat file they are soldered together and a small ring soldered on the flat between the top curves to take the safety chain then the hasp fitted as for the silver one on page 114.

Charms. Most of these are now cast but there are a lot of thin walled items that can be made more competitively with sheet, dies and a little handwork and many of these can be used as earrings as well. One such is the little scimitar shown at fig. 72. The die is pierced out of 3mm silver steel and the punch sawn from the same material and screwed to a mild steel shank. The guard is just a strip with a slot sawn in it centrally for two thirds of its length then slid on to the body and the two tails pressed together and soldered with enough solder to attach it and fill the slot as well. The end of a very

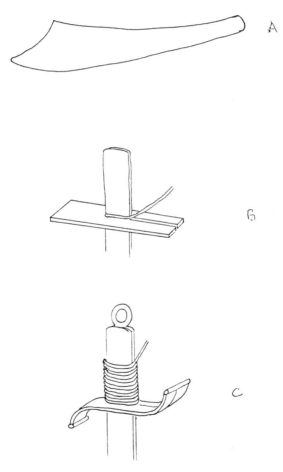

72   Method of making a small scimitar charm

fine wire is also soldered (see 72B) then wrapped around the handle completely covering it then soldered at the top at the same time as the loop is attached. Its appearance is improved if a thin line is wriggled along the short edge of the blade and twisted wire used for the handle.

If a blanking die and punch is made to produce a small anchor in proportion to the cross and heart the three can be hung together to make a Faith, Hope and Charity charm and the anchor too does not look out of place as an earring. The hooks of the anchor would not have to be pronounced or they tend to hook into every piece of material they come into contact with.

A small bell can also serve this dual purpose but these are a little more difficult to make because they are similar in shape to the thimble. Because it is not as deep and narrow as a thimble it can be drawn quite successfully which eliminates the string of dies needed for the thimble. You will have to decide on the precise thickness of the sheet you will use and stick to this every time you make any.

To begin with you will need a circular blank 18mm in diameter. For the drawing die you will need two pieces of flat, bright mild steel bar, 35 or 40mm wide and 4 or 5mm thick. Cut off 80mm for the bottom of the die and 50mm for the top. The bottom piece has to be mounted in the four-jaw chuck and a shallow recess turned in the centre which is just deep enough to accept the circular blank. File any burrs off the blank and place it in the recess and run a finger tip over the two; you can detect extremely minute differences in this way. When you can feel no difference drill an 8mm diameter hole in the centre. To make certain it is dead centre start it with a centre drill. This will be the maximum diameter of the body of the bell.

To form the mouth of the bell round off the edge of the hole and give that, the inside of the hole and the disc recess a smooth finish with fine emery paper. You may have to increase the degree of rounding of the hole later if the gold will not draw in properly.

It is next taken out of the chuck and the two pieces held together and in line with an equal amount of the bottom piece projecting either end of top piece and clamped securely in a hand vice and a hole of about 3mm drilled through the two, centrally side to side and about 1cm from the end of the top piece. The hole in the bottom plate is then tapped to take a screw and the top one enlarged enough for the screw to pass through. The two plates are now screwed together and the same thing done to the other end so that you have two screws holding them firmly together. They are next put in the machine vice on the drilling machine table and the 8mm hole drilled through the top plate using the hole in the bottom plate to guide and position it precisely. This hole will have to be enlarged later to admit the body of the punch. Remove any burr from the hole in the top plate and smooth the side that is in contact with the bottom plate with fine emery paper. A blank is placed in the recess and a punch passes through the hole in the top plate, presses on the blank and 'draws' it through the hole in the bottom plate, hence the term drawing die and the reason for all the smoothness: unnecessary friction has to be reduced to an absolute minimum.

The accuracy of the recess is important because you must prevent wrinkles being formed in the periphery of the blank as this will cause it to jam and the punch to pierce the metal. Surprisingly it is better to be a fraction too tight than too loose.

The shape of the punch must conform to the shape of the finished bell except that the end i.e. the top of the bell, must be flat otherwise most of the pressure will be concentrated in one small area and a fracture will occur. The body of the punch must be a sliding fit in the hole in the top plate; this is used to centre the punch in the die before the blank is inserted. The flat end of the bell can be domed afterwards in a doming block with a doming punch. A cross sectional drawing is shown at fig. 73A.

It is better to use this die in the Pinfold or similar small screw press so you can feel as well as see what is happening. The die is clamped in the press by the extensions on the bottom plate after being centred with the punch. Then the annealed blank, smeared with graphite grease or Vaseline is clamped between the die plates. The punch is forced down until it comes to a stop then given a final tweak to iron out any unevenness that may have formed around the mouth of the bell, then withdrawn. Both screws are then loosened and one removed so the bell can be taken out and a new blank inserted.

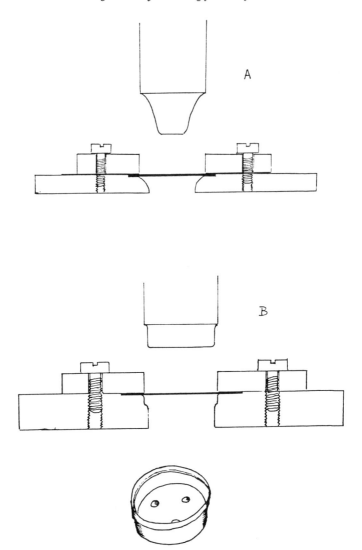

73 'A' Punch and die plate for shaping a bell and 'B' a shallow cup

The clapper is made from a short length of wire with one end melted into a bead and the other turned into a loop with the round nosed pliers. Another piece of wire has a loop turned in it and this loop passed through the one on the clapper and closed. After the end of the bell has been domed a small hole is drilled in the centre of the dome and the free end of the wire threaded through the hole from inside the bell and a loop turned on the other end to keep it in place and to take a jump ring.

This method can be used to form any cup whose height is not greater than its diameter but this rule can vary according to the thickness and type of the metal used.

Another charm that can be made in this way is a little ball game. This is a flat bottomed cup with three recesses pressed into the bottom on the inside. Three loose beads, ball bearings or undrilled pearls are placed inside and a transparent cover fixed into the top.

The only difference between making the die and punch for this and those for the bell is the size of the blank. The cup needs to be about 12mm in diameter and deep enough so that the transparent cover just clears the beads when it is resting on its seating. The seating is formed turning the opening of the lower die plate .5mm larger and to a depth to match the thickness of the cover and a mating ridge turned on the punch. See fig. 73B.

The crown of a small bowler hat can be formed in this way. Given a crease across the top by tapping it with a knife blade it becomes a trilby and turn up one side of the brim and it is an Australian soldier's hat.

The making of a small cigarette lighter uses this principle also. A glance at fig. 74 will show what is needed. The shallow end caps for the body of the lighter will form quite easily without the use of a top plate on the die. A piece of brass or steel rod is used to shape the body strip. The strip is bent into a 'U' and, with the rod inside the 'U', is forced into a matching groove and the top ends of the 'U' bent into position using a steel pusher fixed into a graver handle. When taken out of the groove the body will open up slightly but the end caps will keep it in place while it is being soldered.

The two pieces for the top are formed as one piece in a small drawing die then sawn apart with a piercing saw. A 'U' shaped piece of strip is soldered to the top of the body to take the pivot. The piece that the thumb presses on has a stem soldered inside which passes through a hole in the body. A short piece of spiral watch bracelet spring is first threaded on to the stem so that it returned after it is pressed. A little plaque or

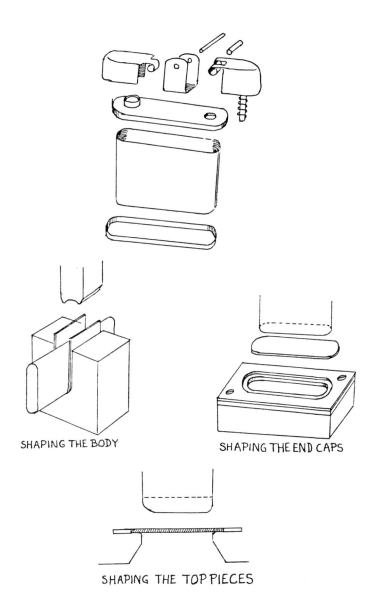

SHAPING THE BODY

SHAPING THE END CAPS

SHAPING THE TOP PIECES

74 The components of a miniature cigarette lighter and the forming dies for shaping them

engraved rectangle on the side of the body will give it a finishing touch.

The picture of the engraving templates on page 63, shows a circle with GOOD LUCK engraved on it. In case you have not come across them there are several charms in the shape of a disc that is held in a semi-circle of strip by two pivots. On the circle are what appear to be hieroglyphics but when the disc is set spinning with a flick of the finger they become readable and say such things as GOOD LUCK, HAPPY BIRTHDAY and so on.

The discs are a straight forward blanking job and for simplicity the small pivots can be soldered on afterwards then, to begin with, you can probably use a blank from a punch and die already made for something else.

The letters of the engraving are divided vertically in half and one half engraved on one side of the disc and the other half on the other side. The problem is to get them perfectly lined up so that they merge correctly when the disc is set spinning. This is done by making a template of the lettering complete then resetting the engraving cutter depth stop so that it cuts as deep again and re-engraving one half of each letter at this depth.

When the disc is mounted in the vice, using the diamond point, engrave all the shallow halves of the letters on one side, turn the disc over (vertically, not side to side) and engrave the deep halves on that side. It could be done by fitting stops in the centre of each letter to limit the movement of the stylus but if your concentration is interrupted it is easy to switch to the wrong side of the letter and not realise it until you come to spin the disc and find you have the same half of a letter engraved on both sides of the disc.

'Good Luck', 'Happy Birthday' and 'I Love You' are well catered for but by making them this way a template can be made in a matter of minutes for wording with a more limited demand but none the less profitable for a small manufacturer.

A small garden roller can be made from two flat bottomed cups soldered together, drilled centrally and a wire handle fitted.

The same two cups soldered together then a narrow slot cut lengthways forms the main part of a whistle. A mouthpiece is made from two pieces of sheet and soldered to one side of the

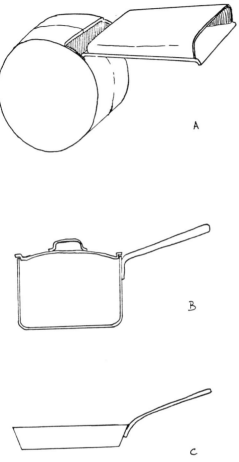

75   Whistle, saucepan and frying pan charms

slot as shown in fig. 75A. By bending the mouthpiece up or down the whistle can be made to work.

A larger cup with a handle and lid joined by a small safety chain would make a saucepan. 75B.

A small circular blank could be turned into the bowl of a frying pan with the use of a very simple forming die. 75C.

Traditional Birthstones

Month	Stone
January	Garnet
February	Amethyst
March	Aquamarine, Bloodstone
April	Diamond, White Sapphire
May	Emerald, Green Spinel
June	Pearl, Moonstone, Alexandrite
July	Ruby
August	Sardonyx, Peridot
September	Sapphire, Blue Spinel
October	Opal, Tourmaline, Rose Beryl
November	Topaz, Citrine, Golden Sapphire
December	Turquoise, Lapis, Zircon

Useful Addresses

Tools
Proops Brothers Ltd
Technology House
34 Saddington Road
Fleckney
Leicester LE8 8AW
Tel. 0116 2 403400

Tools, findings, bullion
Exchange Findings
81 Caroline Street
Hockley
Birmingham B3 1UP
Tel. 0121 236 5211

Bullion
Johnson Matthey PLC
43 Hatton Garden
London EC1N 8EE
Tel. 0171 269 8103

Gemstones
Ruppenthal (UK) Ltd
20/24 Kirby Street
Hatton Garden
London EC1N 8TS
Tel. 0171 405 8068

E.A. Thomson (Gems) Ltd
Chapel House
Hatton Place
Hatton Garden
London EC1N 8RU
Tel. 0171 242 3181

Lathe and machine tools, etc
H.S. Walsh & Sons Ltd
243 Beckenham Road
Kent BR3 4TS
Tel. 0181 778 7061

Birmingham showroom:
1–2 Warstone Mews
Warstone Lane
Birmingham B18 6JB
Tel. 0121 236 9346

R.A. Atkins Ltd
Hunts Hill House
Hunts Hill
Normandy
Guildford
Surrey GU23 2AH

Axminster Power Tool
  Centre
Chard Street
Axminster
Devon EX13 5DZ
Tel. 01297 33656

Chronos Ltd
95 Victoria Street
St Albans
Herts AL1 3TJ

Essel Engineering
23 Cavell Road
Billericay
Essex CM11 2HR

Graham Engineering
  (Midlands) Ltd
Alpine House
Roebuck Lane
West Bromwich
West Midlands B70 6QP
Tel. 0121 525 3133

John Hall (Tools) Ltd
73 North Road
Cardiff CF1 3TF

A.J. Reeves & Co.
  (Birmingham) Ltd
Holly Lane
Marston Lane
Birmingham B37 7AW
Tel. 0121 779 6831

Shesto Ltd
Unit 2, Sapcote Trading
  Centre
374 High Road
Willesden
London NW10 2DH
Tel. 0181 451 6188

Southern Watch & Clock
  Supplies Ltd
Precista House
48–56 High Street
Orpington
Kent BR6 0JH
Tel. 01689 824318

Signs of the Zodiac

Aries the Ram (March 21)

Taurus the Bull (April 20)

Gemini the Twins (May 21)

Cancer the Crab (June 21)

Leo the Lion (July 23)

Virgo the Virgin (August 23)

Libra the Balance (Sept 23)

Scorpio the Scorpion (Oct 23)

Sagittarius the Archer (Nov 20)

Capricorn the Goat (Dec 21)

Aquarius the Water Bearer (Jan 20)

Pisces the Fishes (Feb 18)

DECIMAL AND METRIC EQUIVALENTS
OF COMMON FRACTIONS

Fractions of an inch	Decimals of an inch	Equivalent in millimetres	Fractions of an inch	Decimals of an inch	Equivalent in millimetres
1/64	·01562	·397	33/64	·51562	13·097
1/32	·03125	·794	17/32	·53125	13·494
3/64	·04687	1·191	35/64	·54687	13·891
1/16	·0625	1·588	9/16	·5625	14·288
5/64	·07812	1·984	37/64	·57812	14·684
3/32	·09375	2·381	19/32	·59375	15·081
7/64	·10937	2·778	39/64	·60937	15·478
1/8	·1250	3·175	5/8	·625	15·875
9/64	·14062	3·572	41/64	·64062	16·272
5/32	·15625	3·969	21/32	·65625	16·669
11/64	·17187	4·366	43/64	·67187	17·066
3/16	·1875	4·763	11/16	·6875	17·463
13/64	·20312	5·159	45/64	·70312	17·859
7/32	·21875	5·556	23/32	·71875	18·256
15/64	·23437	5·953	47/64	·73437	18·653
1/4	·2500	6·350	3/4	·75	19·050
17/64	·26562	6·747	49/64	·76562	19·447
9/32	·28125	7·144	25/32	·78125	19·844
19/64	·29687	7·541	51/64	·79687	20·241
5/16	·3125	7·938	13/16	·8125	20·638
21/64	·32812	8·334	53/64	·82812	21·034
11/32	·34375	8·731	27/32	·84375	21·431
23/64	·35937	9·128	55/64	·85937	21·828
3/8	·3750	9·525	7/8	·875	22·225
25/64	·39062	9·922	57/64	·89062	22·622
13/32	·40625	10·319	29/32	·90625	23·019
27/64	·42187	10·716	59/64	·92187	23·416
7/16	·4375	11·113	15/16	·9375	23·813
29/64	·45312	11·509	61/64	·95312	24·209
15/32	·46875	11·906	31/32	·96875	24·606
31/64	·48437	12·303	63/64	·98437	25·003
1/2	·5	12·700	1	1·000	25·400

WHITWORTH STANDARD THREADS
AND BRITISH STANDARD FINE

Diameter Inches	Threads per inch		Root Dia.	Tap Drill Size
	Whit.	B.S.F.		
1/16	60	—	·0412	56
3/32	48	—	·0671	49
1/8	40	—	·0930	40
5/32	32	—	·1162	31
3/16	24	—	·1341	28
7/32	24	—	·1654	18
1/4	20	—	·1860	11
1/4	—	26	·2001	5
9/32	20	—	·2172	2
9/32	—	26	·2321	B
5/16	18	—	·2414	D
5/16	—	22	·2543	G
3/8	16	—	·2950	N
3/8	—	20	·3110	O
7/16	14	—	·3460	S
7/16	—	18	·3665	3/8
1/2	12	—	·3933	X
1/2	—	16	·4200	7/16
9/16	12	—	·4558	15/32
9/16	—	16	·4825	1/2
5/8	11	—	·5086	33/64
5/8	—	14	·5336	35/64
11/16	11	—	·5711	37/64
11/16	—	14	·5961	39/64
3/4	10	—	·6219	5/8
3/4	—	12	·6434	21/32
13/16	10	—	·6844	11/16
13/16	—	12	·7059	23/32
7/8	9	—	·7327	47/64
7/8	—	11	·7586	49/64
15/16	9	—	·7952	13/16
15/16	—	11	·8215	53/64
1	8	—	·8399	27/32
1	—	10	·8720	7/8

DECIMAL EQUIVALENTS OF DRILL SIZES

NUMBER DRILLS

Drill	Equivalent In.	Drill	Equivalent In.
80	·013	44	·086
79½	·0135	43	·089
79	·014	42	·0935
78½	·0145	41	·096
78	·015	40	·098
77	·016	39	·0995
76	·018	38	·1015
75	·020	37	·104
74½	·021	36	·1065
74	·022	35	·110
73½	·0225	34	·111
73	·023	33	·113
72	·024	32	·116
71½	·025	31	·120
71	·026	30	·1285
70	·027	29	·136
69½	·028	28	·1405
69	·029	27	·144
68½	·02925	26	·147
68	·030	25	·1495
67	·031	24	·152
66	·032	23	·154
65	·033	22	·157
64	·035	21	·159
63	·036	20	·161
62	·037	19	·166
61	·038	18	·1695
60½	·039	17	·173
60	·040	16	·177
59	·041	15	·180
58	·042	14	·182
57	·043	13	·185
56	·0465	12	·189
55	·052	11	·191
54	·055	10	·1935
53	·0595	9	·196
52	·0635	8	·199
51	·067	7	·201
50	·070	6	·204
49	·073	5	·2055
48	·076	4	·209
47	·0785	3	·213
46	·081	2	·221
45	·082	1	·228

LETTER DRILLS

Letter	Equivalent
A	0·234
B	·238
C	·242
D	·246
E	·250
F	·257
G	·261
H	·266
I	·272
J	·277
K	·281
L	·290
M	·295
N	·302
O	·316
P	·323
Q	·332
R	·339
S	·348
T	·358
U	·368
V	·377
W	·386
X	·397
Y	·404
Z	·413

Number

BRITISH ASSOCIATION STANDARD THREADS

Number	Pitch mm.	Outside Diameter Inches	Tap Drill Size	Clearance Drill Size
0	1·000	·236	12	B
1	·900	·208	19	3
2	·810	·185	26	$\frac{3}{16}$
3	·730	·161	29	19
4	·660	·142	33	27
5	·590	·126	39	30
6	·530	·110	43	34
7	·480	·098	47	39
8	·430	·087	50	43
9	·390	·075	$\frac{1}{16}$	48
10	·350	·067	54	50
11	·310	·059	56	53
12	·280	·051	61	55

Index

ANTIQUE & TWENTIETH CENTURY JEWELLERY
Vivienne Becker
'Probably the best book on the subject to set out with.'
Options
'An invaluable aid to the novice as well as the expert.'
Financial Times
0 7198 0171 0   250 × 190mm   356pp   78 col. & 270 b/w illus.

JEWELRY CONCEPTS AND TECHNOLOGY   *Oppi Untracht*
This is the definitive guide and handbook for jewellery makers on all levels of ability. Supplemented by an extensive index, glossaries of jewellery forms and findings, it is indispensable for anyone interested in any aspect of jewellery making.
0 7091 9616 4   280 × 220mm   840pp   col. & b/w illus. throughout

JEWELLERY MAKING FOR PROFIT   *J.E. Hickling*
Here, for the first time, is a book that tells you how to go about making jewellery for profit. Written by an expert craftsman, with a lifetime's experience, this book is destined to become the standard work on the subject.
0 7198 0092 7   216 × 138mm   176pp   75 line & 6 b/w illus.

JEWELLERY MANUFACTURE AND REPAIR
Charles A. Jarvis
This is the definitive book for the beginner who wishes to progress to a high standard of jewellery manufacture and repair, as well as for the reader who wishes to earn a living at the craft.
0 7198 0052 8   210 × 150mm   224pp   286 line drawings

METAL TECHNIQUES FOR CRAFTSMEN   *Oppi Untracht*
'It is refreshing to see a new, most comprehensive book on craft techniques. This book is of considerable value and usefulness: interestingly written with many unusual illustrations.'
Design
0 7091 0723 4   265 × 180mm   509pp   b/w illus. throughout

PRACTICAL JEWELLERY REPAIR   *James Hickling*
A really practical textbook for the amateur restorer of jewellery, as well as the working professional and apprentice. There is a very thorough grounding in the various processes and materials required, including working with precious metals and solders.
0 7198 0082 X   230 × 150mm   208pp   200 line drawings

WORKING IN PRECIOUS METALS   *Ernest A. Smith*
'An important book . . . that will inform and interest both professional and lay student.'
Antique Dealer and Collectors' Guide
The book is of exceptional value to the working craftsman and teacher because it explains thoroughly the implications of metallurgical and chemical theory for techniques of metal working.
0 7198 0032 3   210 × 140mm   414pp   20 b/w illus.